France

CHEVALIERS DE MALTE
127
CAVEAU

France

By Don Nardo

Enchantment of the World
Second Series

Children's Press®
An Imprint of Scholastic Inc.
New York Toronto London Auckland Sydney
Mexico City New Delhi Hong Kong
Danbury, Connecticut

Frontispiece: A blue building, Haut-Rhin, Alsace

Consultant: Lauren Wiebe, Professor of French and Spanish, Ohio Wesleyan University, Delaware, Ohio

Please note: All statistics are as up-to-date as possible at the time of publication.

Book production by Herman Adler

Library of Congress Cataloging-in-Publication Data

Nardo, Don, 1947–
France / by Don Nardo.
p. cm.—(Enchantment of the world. Second series)
Includes bibliographical references and index.
Summary: Describes the geography, plants, animals, history, economy, language, sports, arts, religions, culture, and people of France.
ISBN-13: 978-0-516-25948-2
ISBN-10: 0-516-25948-2
1. France—Juvenile literature. I. Title. II. Series.
DC17.N37 2007
944—dc22 2006100706

Published simultaneously in Canada.
Printed in the United States of America. 44

1 2 3 4 5 6 7 8 9 10 R 17 16 15 14 13 12 11 10 09 08

France

Contents

Cover photo:
Town of
Roquebrune

Saint-Tropez

Statue of Vercingétorix

Making France Possible

SOME COUNTRIES HAVE A BIRTHDAY, AN EVENT THAT signaled the beginning of the nation. The United States, for example, counts its nationhood from the time the Declaration of Independence was signed in 1776. But when was France founded? There is no clear date or event that marks its beginning. Instead, the French nation, the French identity, developed gradually over the centuries. Certain events do stand out, however, as crucial in the establishment of France. One of these milestones occurred in the early 700s, when Charles Martel saved France—and Europe—from impending catastrophe.

Opposite: **Angers Castle in the Loire Valley dates back to the 1200s.**

Many French towns are surrounded by thick walls that were built to keep out invaders.

A Dire Threat

Charles Martel means "Charles the Hammer." He earned the nickname for his strength and courage. Charles was the leading Frankish noble of the early 700s. The Franks were a Germanic tribe who had moved into what is now France in the late 400s. At the time, France was not yet a clearly defined country. The Frankish realm was more a collection of estates ruled by local lords. When France's first great national crisis loomed, it happened that Charles was the strongest of the Frankish lords.

Charles Martel was perhaps the greatest general of the Middle Ages. He is admired for his careful preparation, innovative battle plans, and ability to change tactics quickly.

This turned out to be fortunate for the Franks and for all future French people, because the threat that the Franks faced required a forceful response. In the 600s, the new religion of Islam had begun in Arabia. Its followers were called Muslims.

Arab armies soon conquered much of the Middle East, spreading Islam. They then swept across North Africa and crossed over into Spain, where they set up a Muslim realm in A.D. 711. Then the invaders set their sights on the rest of Europe and crossed the Pyrenees Mountains into Frankish territory. For a while, the Arabs were successful. They burned and terrorized villages as they moved northward. By 725, they had reached the town of Autun, about 200 miles (300 kilometers) southeast of Paris. The following year, they took Nîmes, in what is now southeastern France.

Coming Together

During these early years of the Arab conquest, the Frankish nobles were not united. This left them unable to defend themselves. They needed a single leader—someone they all respected—to rally behind. Charles Martel turned out to be that leader. In 732, Charles prepared a large army of Frankish soldiers for battle. He also obtained the support of several thousand warriors from the Burgundians, another group that lived in what is now France.

Charles Martel adopted the bold strategy of seeking out the enemy and attacking, rather than waiting for the enemy to arrive. At the time, the Arab soldiers had just captured Poitiers, in west-central France, and were heading toward Tours to the north. Somewhere between Poitiers and Tours, Charles intercepted the Arabs, and the battle was on.

A Decisive Victory

Charles had his foot soldiers form a gigantic square and protect themselves with a wall of shields and spears. The enemy fighters were unable to break through the shield wall, and both the foot soldiers and the mounted warriors wreaked havoc on those who tried. Eventually, the Arabs retreated to their camp. The Franks then surrounded them and renewed the attack, slaying thousands of soldiers.

When the dust of the great battle had cleared, the Franks rejoiced. The Arab invaders had been so soundly beaten that those who survived retreated south to their Spanish stronghold, never to return.

Charles Martel led an army of about thirty thousand at the Battle of Tours. His men defeated a Muslim army estimated at eighty thousand.

It was one of the most decisive battles in world history. Charles Martel and his men kept Europe from Muslim domination. They also preserved the Frankish realm, creating the foundation for a strong, centralized French nation. In a very real sense, they made France possible. Moreover, in their show of unity and mutual defense, the heroes of the Battle of Tours helped to establish a proud identity for the French nation that was to come.

A Pleasant Land

France is the largest country in western Europe, covering an area almost as big as the U.S. state of Texas. In the north of France are the picturesque beaches of Calais and Dunkerque. Nearly 600 miles (1,000 km) to the south are the rugged Pyrenees Mountains that mark the border with Spain. In between are fertile farmlands, meandering rivers, and rocky

Opposite: **Steep, rocky slopes are common in the Pyrenees.**

Cliffs rise from the sea along the English Channel in northern France.

highlands. The island of Corsica, which lies off the southeastern coast, is also French territory.

Several nations share borders with France. To the east are Italy, Switzerland, and Germany, while Luxembourg and Belgium are to the northeast. Along with Spain, the tiny nations of Andorra and Monaco touch France in the south. France also borders the Atlantic Ocean, the English Channel, and the Mediterranean Sea.

France's Geographic Features

Area: 212,918 square miles (551,458 sq km)

Highest Elevation: Mont Blanc, 15,771 feet (4,807 m)

Lowest Elevation: Sections of the Rhône River, 7 feet (2 m) below sea level

Longest River: Loire, 634 miles (1,020 km)

Largest Lake: Lac du Bourget, 16.6 square miles (43 sq km)

Length of Coastline: 2,129 miles (3,427 km)

Highest Average Temperature: Nice (on Mediterranean coast) 81°F (27°C) in July

Lowest Average Temperature: Briançon (in French Alps), 28°F (–2°C) in January

From Paris to London in Three Hours

In 1994, the completion of a mammoth construction project made headlines around the world. For more than a century, people had been talking about building a tunnel beneath the English Channel, which separates England from France. In 1994, the tunnel finally opened. At first, it was best known by its nickname, "the Chunnel," but today most people call it the Channel Tunnel. It stretches for 31 miles (50 km) from Calais, in northern France, to Folkestone, in southern England. About 24 miles (39 km) of the Channel Tunnel are underwater. Using the tunnel, a traveler can make it from Paris to London in just three hours.

The Paris Basin

France is both large and diverse. It features three major kinds of landforms. The first is lowland basins, which include the valleys of the Loire, Seine, Rhône, and Garonne rivers. Over the ages, the rivers have deposited enormous amounts of sediment on the nearby land. This has created rich farmlands in these basins.

The Paris Basin is fertile and mild. It is filled with pleasant towns like Bourg d'Iré.

The largest and most productive of France's lowland basins is the Paris Basin, in the north-central section of France. This huge, saucer-shaped region covers about one-fifth of the country. The capital city of Paris is near its center. Throughout history, the Paris Basin has been the most populated part of France.

It is easy to see why people have always been attracted to the Paris Basin. For one thing, it has a pleasant climate. The winters are cool but rarely cold, and the summers are long and warm. The average temperature across north-central France in July is a comfortable 75 degrees Fahrenheit (24 degrees Celsius). More importantly, the region's fertile soil is good for growing crops and raising livestock. Most of the country's industry and economic activity is located in the Paris Basin.

The World's Wine Capital

Bordeaux is France's ninth-largest city and one of its oldest. The site of Bordeaux, on the Garonne River, was occupied from 300 B.C. by Celtic tribesmen. The Romans took charge of the town around 60 B.C., and it thrived until it was sacked by invaders in the third century and again in the fifth century. Bordeaux revived in medieval times, and a large cathedral was erected there in about A.D. 1100. After that, the city continued to grow and prosper.

Renowned for its architectural beauty, Bordeaux is particularly famous for the *Esplanade des Quinconces*, the largest town square in Europe. In the 1700s, architects rebuilding parts of Paris used Boudeaux as a model.

Today, the city is most famous for its wine. It supports some thirteen thousand grape growers and every other year hosts the Vinexpo, the world's largest event for wine growers, buyers, and distributors.

Biarritz in the Aquitaine Basin was founded as a whaling village more than a thousand years ago. By the 1800s, it was a popular vacation spot.

Pleasant Plains and Valleys

France has several other lowland basins and gently rolling plains, each dominated by a major river system. One of these, the Alsace Plain, lies east of the Paris Basin along the Rhine River, the boundary between France and Germany. The Alsace region is renowned for its grapes, which are used to make fine wines, especially white wines.

The Aquitaine Basin lies along the Atlantic coast. The peaceful Garonne River winds through the Aquitaine lowlands, which feature alternating patches of lush rolling farmland and shady groves of pine trees. This region, too, is known for its wine grapes, particularly around Bordeaux.

The ocean waters that border the Aquitaine are mild. As a result, the region has a temperate climate characterized by

Saint-Tropez is one in a line of resort towns along the Mediterranean. Its waters are sometimes crowded with yachts and sailboats.

mild winters and cool but still pleasant summers. This climate extends up the coast into the region known as Brittany, which juts like a huge thumb out into the Atlantic.

In central France lies a long, narrow, fertile valley called the Rhône–Saône Corridor. This valley stretches north to south for more than 250 miles (400 km) along the Rhône and Saône rivers. In the heart of the valley, amid green plains dotted by fruit orchards, vegetable gardens, and vineyards, stands Lyon, France's third-largest city. Not surprisingly, Lyon is filled with factories for processing and packing crops.

The Sunny Mediterranean Coast

The Rhône empties into the Mediterranean Sea. The French call the region just east of the Rhône the Côte d'Azur, or "Sky Blue Coast." Many foreigners know the area as the French Riviera. Local and foreign tourists flock to the Côte d'Azur to enjoy its warm waters and weather. The Côte d'Azur has hot, dry summers and mild, humid winters. For instance, the city of Marseille has an average high temperature of 83°F (28°C) in August. It rains an average of sixty days a year in Marseille, totaling only about 22 inches (56 centimeters). The Sun shines most of the rest of the time.

This almost ideal climate prevails along the coast east of Marseille, including the famous resort towns of Toulon, Saint-Tropez, Cannes, and Nice. All boast beautiful beaches frequented by sunbathers. Cannes is also renowned for its film festival, which attracts movie stars from around the world.

The Cannes Film Festival

Every year top filmmakers from around the globe come to Cannes to take part in the world's most famous and prestigious film festival. The festival, which was established in 1946, lasts two weeks. Filmmakers from dozens of countries submit their works, hoping to gain recognition and win a prize. The grand prize, the Palme d'Or ("Golden Palm"), is awarded for best film. The Cannes judges also hand out prizes for best actor, actress, director, and screenplay.

France's "Natural Fortress"

France's second major landform consists of its highland plateaus. These rugged, rocky regions rise a few hundred or thousand feet above sea level. They are the remnants of ancient mountain ranges that wind, rain, and sun have worn down over millions of years. The highland plateaus typically consist of steep, jagged hillsides and ravines dotted with small trees and bushes. They are wild and hard to cross, and few people live there.

The largest highland plateau in France is the Massif Central. Sandwiched between the Aquitaine Basin and the Rhône–Saône Valley, it occupies most of south-central France.

A row of extinct volcanoes rises in Auvergne Volcanoes National Park in the Massif Central.

The Loire River is the longest river in France. It is famous for the many castles along its route.

The plateau's outer fringes are less than 1,000 feet (300 meters) high, but much of the central portion rises to more than 5,000 feet (1,500 m). Its rugged cliffs, gorges, and other rocky formations have inspired some writers to call this region France's "central natural fortress."

The climate in the Massif Central is more extreme than in the lowlands. In the summer, sudden—and often destructive—thunderstorms whip across the plateau. Winters are cold, averaging about 30°F (–1°C). Snow often blankets the region, blocking roads for several months and making it difficult or impossible to reach remote areas.

When these snows melt in the spring, they feed the plateau's hundreds of small mountain streams. These streams converge to form the sources for several of France's major rivers, including the Loire and the Vienne.

The town of Le Puy-en-Veley spreads out around an ancient church that sits atop a rocky hill. The town has been an important Christian site for at least 1,600 years.

Because of its difficult terrain and sometimes harsh climate, the Massif Central has few large towns or major roads. Many of the roads zigzag through the bottoms of chasms or snake back and forth along the sides of steep hills or cliffs. Driving on them can be frightening, especially when only a few inches of pavement separate your car from a sheer drop. The hair-raising drive is usually worth it, however, because the view from the top can be breathtaking.

The Massif Central's rugged, rocky terrain also makes farming difficult. Here and there, in small sheltered valleys nestled between huge boulders and cliffs, villagers tend small crops of corn and vegetables or raise sheep and goats. These farms are very different from those in the more fertile river valleys, which export a great deal of food to other parts of France and Europe. Most of the food produced on the Massif Central is eaten by people who live there.

A Look at French Cities

Marseille (below), France's second-largest city and biggest commercial port, lies on the Mediterranean coast. It is home to about 800,000 people. Marseilles is an ancient city, established by the Greeks in about 600 B.C. Today, tourists enjoy visiting Marseille's old port, which is flanked by two huge fortresses.

Lyon (above), in south-central France, is the nation's third-largest city, with about 450,000 people. It began as a Gallic village and later became the capital of Rome's Gallic province. Many ancient and medieval buildings still stand in Lyon. Some of them have secret underground passages that were used by freedom fighters evading the Germans during World War II. Modern Lyon boasts many fine shops, restaurants, theaters, and museums.

The fifth-largest French city, Nice, has a population of almost 350,000. It is located near the eastern end of the French Riviera, on the Mediterranean coast. Because Nice is warm in the summer and mild in the winter, it attracts hordes of tourists. They frequent the area beaches and gamble in the city's famed casinos. Another popular tourist attraction in the city is a romantic cliff fortress, the Colline du Château, which was first inhabited more than two thousand years ago.

France's other highland plateaus are smaller than the Massif Central and have lower elevations, so their terrain is less rugged and their climates less harsh. The Armorican Massif is located west of the Paris Basin, while the Ardennes Plateau crosses the border into Belgium and Luxembourg. Still another mountainous plateau, the relatively small Vosges, lies in eastern France between the Paris Basin and the Alsace Plain.

Spectacular Peaks

The third major type of landform in France is towering mountain ranges. The Pyrenees and the French Alps are relatively young as mountains go, so wind, rain, and ice have not yet eroded them. These mountains have many spectacular peaks that soar above the surrounding plateaus and river valleys.

The Pyrenees run east to west along France's southern border with Spain, forming an imposing barrier between the two nations. The range features many snow-covered peaks, several exceeding 10,000 feet (3,000 m) in height. The Pyrenees have almost no low-lying passes. In fact, not a single pass below 5,000 feet (1,500 m) can be found in the range's central section, which stretches 190 miles (300 km). This makes the Pyrenees difficult to cross.

The French Alps, which rise in southeastern France, also have many towering peaks. The highest is Mont Blanc, the tallest mountain in western Europe, which soars to 15,771 feet (4,807 m). Unlike the Pyrenees, the French Alps are broken in places by river valleys, including the Rhône, the Isère, and the Durance. These valleys provide fairly easy access through the Alps to Italy and Switzerland.

The climate in the mountains is generally cold and harsh. In the high mountain valleys, which often contain scattered villages, winters are long and cold and summers short and cool. The town of Briançon, in the Alps near the Italian border, is typical. The average January temperature there is 28°F (–2°C), while in midsummer the thermometer rarely goes above 63°F (17°C). Towns in these high valleys often experience moderate or heavy snowfall on fifty or more days a year.

Briançon is one of the highest cities in Europe.

CHAPTER THREE

Preserving Nature

Hikers trek across the rocky French Alps.

Because France has a diverse array of landscapes, ranging from seacoasts to river valleys to mountain peaks, it boasts a wide variety of plants and animals. France is home to about one hundred species of mammals, fifty species of reptiles and amphibians, and more than three hundred species of birds. The country also supports thousands of species of trees, bushes, vines, and other plants. Most of the species found in France live throughout much of Europe.

Shrinking Habitats

The kind and number of plants and animals in France have changed over time. Some of these changes were caused by natural forces, such as mountain-building and shifts in climate. But most of the changes are the result of human activity.

Opposite: **A stream tumbles down a mountain slope in Vanoise, France's first national park.**

About 10 percent of the trees in French forests are beech.

Thousands of years ago, France was covered in dense forests that were home to a wide variety of plants and animals. Huge bison, wild oxen called aurochs, and lynx (large wildcats) roamed through giant stands of beech and oak trees. Beavers made their homes in sparkling streams where herds of red deer and wild boar stopped to drink. Birds nested in every natural niche, from the marshes along the Rhône River to the rocky crags and ravines of the Massif Central.

Between three thousand and four thousand years ago, when human beings began settling the area on a large scale, the numbers and kinds of plants and animals began to change. This was partly because people hunted animals for food or to use their skins for clothing. In time, such hunting drove the bison, aurochs, and other large animals to extinction.

Human settlers also cleared forests for firewood and to build farms and towns. This destroyed or reduced the size of the natural habitats of many species. With fewer trees to nest in, for example, many types of birds became more scarce or migrated to other parts of Europe. And humans increasingly encroached on or polluted the streams and rivers where beavers lived. At one time, beavers were plentiful in most of France's lowlands and plateaus. Today, only a few beaver remain, and they are protected by law.

The Return of the Beaver

The European beaver is one of France's rarest creatures. The species was once plentiful in France and in many other parts of Europe. But in the eighteenth and nineteenth centuries, trappers killed beavers in huge numbers, partly for their furry pelts and partly to obtain a substance some people used as medicine. Fortunately, the French government began protecting the country's beavers before they became extinct. Today, a number of beaver colonies live along the small rivers that feed into the Rhône.

Troubled Forests

In December 1999, a huge storm struck northern France with winds of 110 miles per hour (175 kph). The whipping winds destroyed 270 million trees.

France's forests were already in trouble before the storm because people had been logging and clearing land for hundreds of years. Today, only about 25 percent of France's land area remains forested.

Fortunately, a large-scale tree-planting program is underway. Its goal is to restore as many of the country's lost trees as possible.

When people cleared the forests, they permanently changed the nature of the land and the plants that thrived there. Many of the lowlands and plains had been covered by thick forests dominated by shade-loving beech trees. When people began cutting down these trees, more light entered the wooded areas. Over time, this caused a drop in the number of beech trees and an increase in the number of oaks, which can tolerate more direct sunlight. People also introduced herds of grazing animals, such as sheep and goats. Centuries of overgrazing turned many once-green forests into open pastures and heath—treeless areas with poor soil.

Protecting Plants and Animals

Eventually, the French began to recognize the importance of preserving the natural environment. Coming up with effective ways of doing it took a long time, however. Royal proclamations designed to protect the forests were issued in 1219, 1515, and 1669. These did little in the short run—and nothing in the long run—to stop the destruction of trees. In 1853, a group of French painters called on the government to create

Tsanteleina is one of many French peaks that tops 11,000 feet (3,500 m).

a nature preserve to protect plants and animals. And in 1901, a few concerned French citizens started a society dedicated to protecting the country's natural heritage.

It was not until the 1960s that the French government began to protect plants and animals on a large scale. In 1966, most of the nation's forests came under the protection of the National Forest Service. And in 1970, the government created the organization that later became the Ministry for the Environment and the Quality of Life.

The village of Tignes le Lavachet serves as a jumping off point for Vanoise National Park. The park is a mix of snowcapped mountains and green valleys.

In the meantime, the government set aside small areas as national parks and nature preserves. The national parks are designed to preserve large tracts of land in their present state, so that people can enjoy what remains of France's natural heritage. France's first national park, the Vanoise, which is located in the Alps, was established in 1963. Later, six more national parks were created.

Many Nature Preserves

During the 1960s and 1970s, France also saw the creation of many small nature preserves. Now numbering 310, these are designed to protect specific kinds of plants or animals that are rare or in danger of disappearing entirely. The largest nature preserve in France is the Camargue, which covers about 52 square miles (135 sq km) near the marshy mouth of the Rhône River. The area is a vital habitat for beavers, badgers, and more than two hundred species of birds. These include egrets, wild ducks, herons, and flamingos. Another nature preserve is the Sept-Îles ("Seven Islands"), a group of tiny islands off the coast of Brittany. Some of these islands are nesting sites for gulls, cormorants, puffins, gannets, oystercatchers, and other birds.

About thirty herds of wild horses live in the Camargue. These horses are a cross between the region's ancient native wild horses and domestic horses that passed through the area hundreds of years ago.

The National Flower

France's national flower is a stylized lily, an elegant symbol known as a *fleur-de-lis*. The symbol first became common in medieval France. At that time, it often appeared on the shields and banners of knights and kings.

Animal Parks

Although many animal species dwell in the wild in France, some live only in the country's zoos, which the French call *parcs zoologiques* ("animal parks"). One of the largest and most popular animal parks in France is the Parc Zoologique des Minières, in Doué-la-Fontaine in the Loire Valley. It features monkeys, deer, and emus—large flightless birds native to Australia. The Parc Zoologique de Clères, in Normandy, has antelopes, kangaroos, monkeys, and more than two hundred species of birds. Larger wild beasts, including elephants, hippopotamuses, camels, zebras, and lions, can be seen in the animal park in Thoiry, a few miles west of Paris. This park gained fame for producing the world's first "ligrons," a cross between lions and tigers.

Houses cluster around a stone bridge near the Normandy Maine park in northern France.

All told, France's national parks and preserves cover about 8 percent of the country. Foreign tourists are often surprised to find that people live in these protected zones. But farms and villages dotted these areas long before they were set aside. In France, only the mountain peaks are completely uninhabited. The people who live in France's parks and preserves are careful to follow the rules set down to protect the wildlife.

Goats graze on the hills of southwestern France. Cheese made from goat's milk is popular in France.

Plants and Animals

Soil quality, rainfall, temperature, and elevation are among the factors that determine which trees and bushes grow in the forests or the countryside. Oak and beech are most common across the lowlands of northern and central France. Hornbeam, a sturdy small tree in the birch family, frequently sprouts beneath the larger oak. In the west and southwest, stands of oak and sweet chestnut are found amid large stretches of maritime pine. Higher altitudes, including sections of the Massif Central, the Pyrenees, and the Alps, have silver fir, spruce, Scotch pine, and larch. In the warm Mediterranean climate of the southeast, cork oak, kermes oak, Aleppo pine, and olive trees thrive.

Domestic livestock are the most common animals in France. In 2005, the country contained about 275 million chickens and other poultry. It also had more than 19 million cattle, 15 million pigs, 9 million sheep, 1.2 million goats, and more than 350,000 horses.

Most of France's wild mammals are found in many parts of Europe, as well as in Asia and North America. These include mice, rats, porcupines, squirrels, and other small creatures. Deer and fox live in the forests, while goatlike chamois live high in the mountains.

France is also home to several kinds of snakes. The largest are the western whip snake and Aesculapian snake. Both can grow to be 7 feet (2 m) long. Other reptiles seen in France include sand lizards and green lizards.

The Aesculapian snake eats lizards when it is young. After it is fully grown, it preys on moles, birds, and other small creatures.

CHAPTER FOUR

Becoming France

THROUGH THE CENTURIES, MANY DIFFERENT PEOPLES lived in the region that is now France. Each one left its mark. This mix slowly but steadily shaped the country's culture and national character. In medieval times, France emerged as a nation, one that was destined to play a key role in the turbulent events of modern world history.

Opposite: **Early French hero Vercingétorix fought the Romans who invaded Gaul.**

A reconstruction of a Cro-Magnon man. Cro-Magnons were an early version of modern humans.

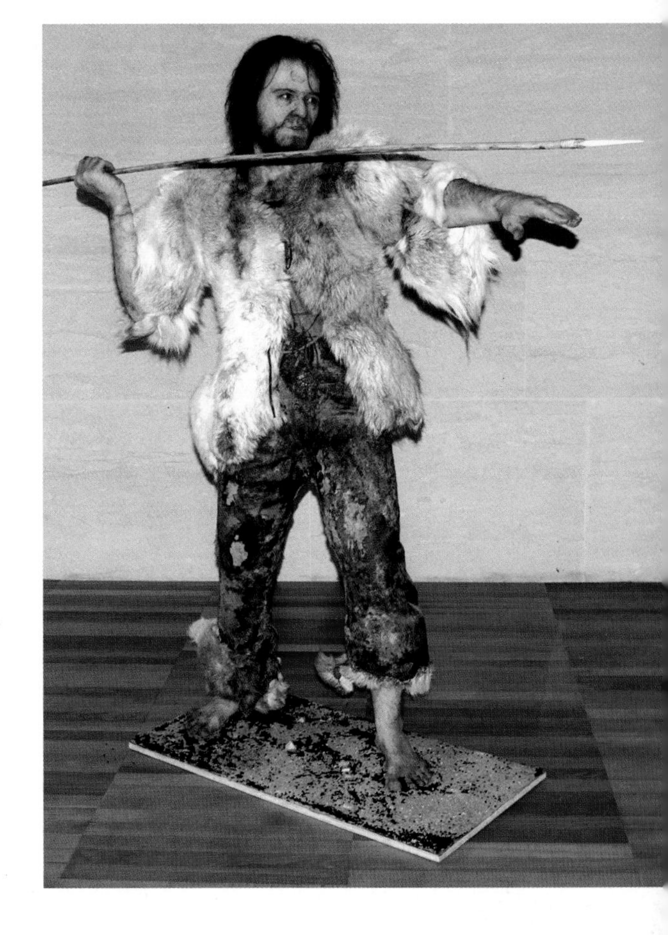

Stone Age France

The first people to inhabit what is now France were Stone Age hunters called Neanderthals. Evidence suggests that tribes of Neanderthals lived in the region at least seventy thousand years ago. Short, stocky, and strong, the Neanderthals were hunter-gatherers who used tools made of stone and animal bones. During cold weather, they camped in caves. There, they built fires to cook meat and to scare off wild animals.

Sometime between thirty thousand and forty thousand years ago, another race of humans arrived in France. They are called Cro-Magnons, after the name of a cave in southern France where scientists first discovered their remains in 1868. Like the Neanderthals, the Cro-Magnons were hunter-gatherers who roamed from place to place, following migrating herds of animals. Animal bones found at Cro-Magnon sites reveal that they regularly stalked and killed large beasts, including mammoths (huge, hairy elephants), reindeer, and horses. The Cro-Magnons also made fantastic cave paintings. The most impressive examples were found in 1940 at Lascaux, in the Aquitaine region east of Bordeaux.

The hunter-gatherer societies living in France changed little over thousands of years. Then, in about 4000 B.C., new peoples arrived in the area. They knew how to grow crops and raise

Stone Age Artists

A sort of Stone Age art museum was discovered in 1940 in the Lascaux Caves, in southwestern France. The caves contain more than 600 paintings along with nearly 1,500 engravings carved into the rock walls. Most of the pictures depict large animals. Others show human handprints. Experts think that these treasures were created by Cro-Magnon artists about seventeen thousand years ago. The cave was opened to the public in 1948, but it was closed in 1963 because the breath and body heat of visitors damaged the paintings. In 1983, a replica of the cave and its artworks, Lascaux II, opened.

livestock. This knowledge was revolutionary. By combining agriculture and hunting, people had a much more reliable food supply than they could get by hunting and gathering alone. Now they were able to settle in one place. They established farms and villages. Another advance occurred in about 2000 B.C., when a new wave of outsiders entered the area that is now France. This group introduced metal tools and weapons, which proved to be much more efficient than those made of stone.

Enter the Celts and Romans

Between 1000 and 750 B.C., tribal peoples collectively known as the Celts migrated to France from central Europe. The Celts were more technically advanced than the tribes already in France. They had horses, which they rode and used to pull carts. They also used wheels and iron tools and weapons. As Celtic civilization spread throughout France, it became more varied. By the first century B.C., more than two hundred different tribes lived in the area. Each had its own customs and territory, which often included villages with strong defensive walls.

Around this time, the Romans, who came from what is now central Italy, began making inroads into France. They referred to the region as "Gaul" and called the Celts "Gauls." The Romans had already carved out a huge empire that included nearly all the lands bordering the Mediterranean Sea. Unlike the scattered Celtic tribes, who had no central government or army, Rome was a well-organized nation with a large and brutally efficient military.

The Earliest French Hero

Vercingétorix, a Celtic chieftain who bravely stood up to Julius Caesar during the Roman conquest of Gaul, is considered France's first national hero. In 52 B.C., Vercingétorix launched a massive rebellion against the Romans, who had recently taken control of most of Gaul. In an incredible display of courage and determination, his warriors fought Caesar nearly to a standstill. The Romans eventually prevailed, however, and Vercingétorix had no choice but to surrender. His patriotism and valor were never forgotten by the people of the region. Today, statues of him can be found all over France.

In 118 B.C., the Romans established a colony on France's southern coast. Greek settlers in the area had long been content to remain on the coast. Except for trading goods, they left the Gauls alone. But the Romans were intent on expanding their empire and their influence. Soon, the Roman colony grew into a large province called Narbonensis.

The Roman intrusion into Gaul became a full-blown conquest about a half century later. In 58 B.C., Roman leader Julius Caesar marched northward from Narbonensis at the head of his army. Over the next six years, Caesar subdued the Gallic tribes one by one, destroying villages, farms, and entire cultures. In all, he fought more than thirty major battles, captured more than eight hundred towns, and killed more than a million Gauls.

After the Romans had conquered Gaul, they began "Romanizing" the remaining Gauls. They taught them to speak Latin, the language of Rome, and to adopt Roman customs and ideas. Meanwhile, thousands of Romans settled in Gaul and, over time, intermarried with the locals. They divided the country into several provinces and built cities, roads, temples, amphitheaters, and bathhouses. Roman ideas and customs took firm root in the area and profoundly shaped the development of French culture.

The Frankish Realm

For several centuries, Gaul thrived as part of the Roman Empire. In the fifth century A.D., however, that empire fell apart as more tribes swept across Europe in search of new living space. Among the new peoples who passed through or settled in Gaul were the Visigoths, the Vandals, and the Burgundians. But the most important were the Franks, who gave their name to the area. In the late 400s, a Frank named Clovis set up the Frankish Kingdom—*regnum Francorum* in Latin. Over time, *Francorum* became *Francia* and, finally, *France*.

Clovis defeated the last great Roman army in Gaul, ending Roman control of the region.

Clovis established the French Merovingian dynasty, or ruling family line, named for his grandfather, Merovech. Because Clovis converted to Christianity, his realm became Christian, and France has remained largely Christian ever since. Clovis made Paris his capital city, helping to establish its long-term importance. When Clovis died in 511, his four sons divided the kingdom among themselves. They and the leaders of the next several generations of Merovingians fought almost continuous civil wars, each attempting to gain control of the whole country for themselves.

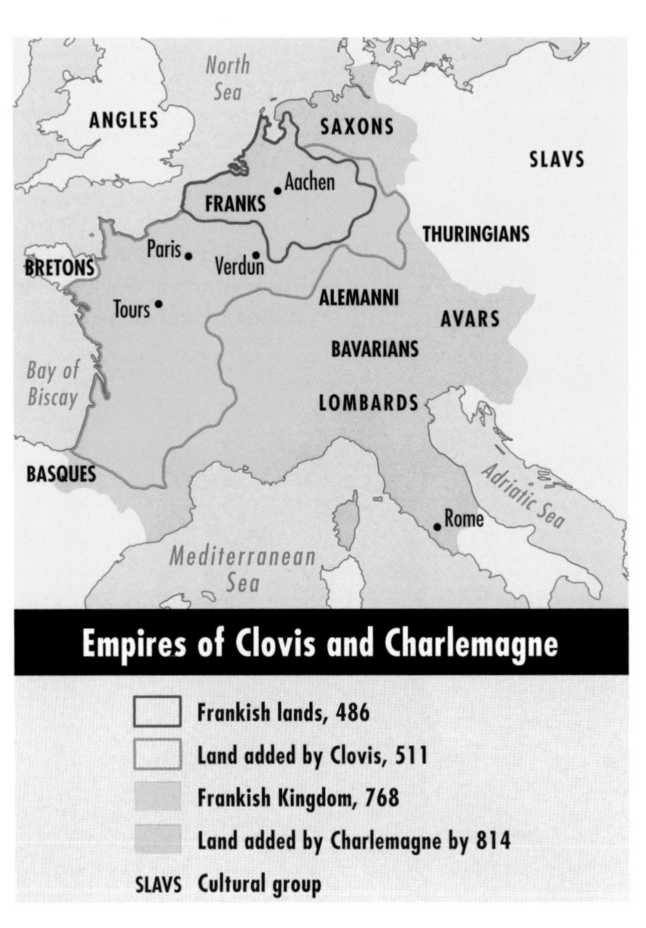

Empires of Clovis and Charlemagne

By the late 600s and early 700s, the Merovingian rulers had become so corrupt and weak that they lost the reins of power to their chief advisors. These were the Carolingians, who soon established their own dynasty. In 732, a Carolingian named Charles Martel saved France (and likely all of Europe) from conquest. Near Tours, in west-central France, he defeated a large army of Muslims who had earlier crossed over from North Africa and taken control of Spain.

Charles Martel's grandson, Charlemagne, engaged in even more ambitious military campaigns. In only a few years, he created an empire that included not only France but also parts of what are now Belgium, Germany, and Italy. In the year 800, Pope Leo III, the head of the Roman Catholic Church, crowned Charlemagne emperor. He and many others believed that Charlemagne was leading a reborn Roman Empire. But this lofty dream came to nothing. After Charlemagne died in 814, his descendants fought among themselves, as Clovis's heirs had done. They carved up the empire into their own little kingdoms, and it fell apart.

Rivalry with England

During the last years of the Carolingian dynasty, the seeds of what would become a long rivalry between France and England were planted. Bands of Norsemen (Vikings) from the area that is now Norway and Denmark had long been raiding northern France. Eventually, the Norsemen sailed up the Seine River and attacked Paris. In 911, Carolingian king, Charles the Simple, made a deal with the Viking leader, Rollo, giving him the region in northwestern France called Normandy. Its people became known as Normans.

In the years that followed, the Normans transformed their small territory into a wealthy, powerful state. Although it was physically part of France, it became more or less a separate kingdom. In 1066, a descendant of Rollo, William I, crossed

The Viking Attack

The Vikings laid siege to Paris in the winter of 885–886. At first, it seemed certain that these fierce warriors from Denmark and Norway would take the city. They tried every way they could think of to get past the city walls into Paris, including using battering rams and tunneling under the walls. But the Parisians managed to counter each kind of attack. The Vikings finally gave up on Paris, although their continued raids into northern France eventually allowed them to gain a foothold there.

English arrows proved brutally effective against French soldiers in the Battle of Crécy. An estimated twelve thousand French were killed.

the English Channel, defeated the English at the Battle of Hastings, and seized control of England. This earned him the nickname "William the Conqueror." The Norman-English rulers who succeeded him held onto their lands in Normandy and even expanded them at the expense of the French kings.

Friction steadily mounted between France and England. Eventually, the French kings tried to expel the English from France. Full-scale war broke out in 1337. It became known as the Hundred Years' War, although it lasted a bit longer than that. Most of the fighting consisted of small-scale raids on enemy towns and villages, although there were a few large battles. In two of theses battles, at Crécy (1346) and Poitiers (1356), the French were caught under a blizzard of arrows unleashed by the English. The French suffered huge losses. Over time, though, they rebounded.

The Naval Battle of Sluys

Naval battles were rare in Europe in medieval times. One of the largest and most decisive was fought in 1340, early in the Hundred Years' War. The French hatched a bold scheme to invade England by crossing the English Channel. To this end, French commanders assembled some two hundred ships at Sluys, in what is now southern Holland. But the English king, Edward III, anticipated this move. He led his own warships across the channel and assaulted the French near Sluys. In a desperate effort to stop the onrushing enemy, the French tied several of their ships together, forming a barrier. It was no use. The English archers killed huge numbers of French sailors and then boarded the French ships. Because of the destruction of the French fleet, most of the war's battles took place in France rather than England.

Joan of Arc

The climax of France's reversal of fortune against the English came in the early 1400s, during the reign of the French king Charles VII. For seventeen years, France had been in a bloody civil war fought by two factions—the Burgundians, who were allied with the English, and the Armagnacs. Charles, the leader of the Armagnacs, was at first at a disadvantage. The English and the Burgundians controlled most of the country. They kept him from reaching Reims, the city in which French kings were officially crowned.

This situation changed in July 1429. The Burgundian soldiers in charge of Reims fled when they heard that Charles VII and his new "champion" were approaching at the head of

Joan of Arc is one of France's greatest heroes. Hundreds of histories, poems, plays, and novels have been written about her.

Crowning a King

After she captured Orléans in May 1429, Joan of Arc and her army marched northward toward Reims, winning more victories along the way. Finally, on July 16, Charles and Joan entered Reims in triumph. The townspeople filled the streets and the town square, loudly cheering and celebrating their liberation. They were awed and thrilled at the unusual sight of a young woman decked out in shining armor, riding a handsome white horse, and carrying a magnificent banner bearing images of Jesus and the angels Michael and Gabriel. The next day—July 17, 1429—Joan knelt beside Charles in the local cathedral. There, a French clergyman crowned him Charles VII, the true king of France.

an army. That champion was a seventeen-year-old girl named Jeanne d'Arc, or Joan of Arc. The young woman claimed that she had recently heard the voices of angels and long-dead Christian saints. The voices, she said, had instructed her to put on armor and free the town of Orléans, which English troops had surrounded. Charles had accepted her story and had given her command of an army. By May 8, 1429, after several furious battles, she had driven the enemy away from Orléans, saving the city.

After Joan and Charles entered Reims, he was crowned king. But thereafter, Joan's own fortunes changed for the worse. She was captured in battle and held prisoner by the Burgundians and the English. They accused her of being a witch, put her on trial, and on May 30, 1431, burned her at the stake.

National Expansion

Despite Joan's tragedy, the revolution she and Charles set in motion could not be stopped. Inspired by her example and sacrifice, the Armagnacs fought on, won victory after victory, and prevailed. In 1435, they signed a treaty with the Burgundians, ending the civil war. Led by Charles, the united French armies drove the English completely out of the country by 1453.

In the following centuries, many French monarchs tried to expand France's power, as well as their own. The French kings increased their own authority by reducing the power of the nobles, who had long ruled their vast estates like tiny kingdoms. Some French kings also fought to obtain more land. For example, Francis I, who ruled from 1515 to 1547, waged numerous wars in Europe. In these conflicts, he won control of important Italian territories and began a long-lasting rivalry between French and German rulers.

Francis I was a great supporter of the arts. He hired the world's best artists, such as Leonardo da Vinci, to work for him.

Francis was also interested in exploring the Western Hemisphere, which Europeans had only recently discovered. Beginning in 1534, Jacques Cartier led three expeditions to what is now southern Canada and traveled up the St. Lawrence River. Based on his travels, the French laid claim to Canada, marking the beginning of France's overseas empire.

France's Greatest King

Perhaps the greatest French king of all was Louis XIV. He ruled from 1643 to 1715, the longest royal reign

The Palace of Versailles

The most lavish royal palace in Europe was built in the late 1600s for Louis XIV. Versailles is located about 11 miles (18 km) southwest of Paris. Roughly thirty-six thousand workers labored for almost thirty years to build the mammoth palace. When the palace was finally completed, it featured a chapel, a theater, an opera house, and quarters for more than ten thousand guests and servants.

in European history. Louis was determined to make France the strongest nation on Earth. He fought four large-scale wars against other European powers, seized land in Italy and the Netherlands, and set up trading posts in North America and India. Louis was also a loyal patron of the arts and learning. His government established schools of painting and sculpture, science, architecture, and music. He also turned a royal hunting lodge into the magnificent Palace of Versailles, near Paris.

Needless to say, Louis's wars, building projects, and lavish lifestyle were not cheap. Much of the money came from taxing France's commoners, the working people who were collectively known as the "third estate." Most belonged to the lowest—and by far the largest—social class, made up of poor peasants, laborers, and craftspeople. The third estate also included a smaller number of slightly better-off shopkeepers, businessmen, lawyers, and doctors. They were the country's middle class. France's second estate consisted of the well-to-do nobility. The Christian clergy made up the first estate. Members of the first and second estates, who together accounted for only about 3 percent of the population, did not have to pay taxes. They enjoyed luxurious lifestyles, largely at the commoners' expense.

A Bloody Revolution

This unfair situation became increasingly unbearable in the years following Louis XIV's death. The next king, Louis XV, wasted large sums of money on personal luxuries. He also waged costly wars, the most devastating being the Seven Years' War (called the French and Indian War in the Americas), which lasted from 1756 to 1763. France was defeated and lost most of its overseas empire, including its North American colonies, to Britain.

Louis XV died in 1774, and another weak and selfish king, Louis XVI, took the throne. The commoners continued to bear the burden of heavy taxes, but the national treasury continued to shrink. By 1787, it was virtually empty, and the country was deep in debt. Social discontent, which had been building for decades, neared the breaking point.

Then, in May 1789, Louis made the mistake of calling a meeting of deputies from each of the country's three estates. He hoped to squeeze more money out of the third estate. But the plan backfired when the delegates suddenly and boldly declared themselves to be France's National Assembly. They demanded that the king draft a new constitution reducing the monarchy's power. When Louis refused, a Paris mob stormed and captured the Bastille, the royal fortress-prison. The French Revolution had begun. The date was July 14, 1789, which the French have celebrated as their independence day ever since.

Over the next ten years, France underwent massive turmoil, bloodshed, and political chaos. The new government abolished the monarchy and declared France a republic (later called the First Republic) in September 1792. Louis was tried for treason and executed four months later. Soon afterward, the government fell into the hands of extremists, and thousands of people were beheaded in what is known as the Reign of Terror. Among them was Louis's wife, Marie Antoinette.

French citizens storm the Bastille. The Bastille had been built as a fort in the 1300s and was converted into a prison in the 1600s.

France Versus Europe

Eventually, the army, led by General Napoléon Bonaparte, stepped in and restored order. But the price of that order was dictatorship. In 1799, Napoléon took over the government, and in 1804, he made himself emperor.

Power over a single country was apparently not enough for Napoléon. He began an aggressive foreign policy and for several years led French armies to victory over the forces of Europe's strongest nations. This resulted in a European empire rivaled only by that

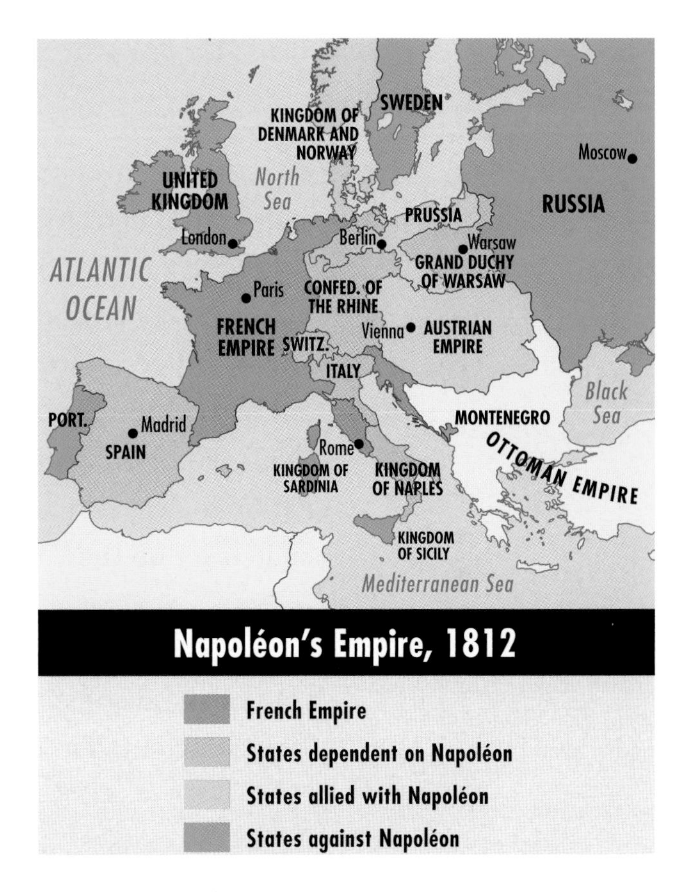

Some experts consider Napoléon the greatest general in world history. He was ruthless, dynamic, and inspiring.

of Charlemagne. Finally, in 1815, the armies of Britain, Prussia, and Austria defeated Napoléon at Waterloo, in Belgium.

The years following Napoléon's defeat were no less turbulent for France. In 1848, Paris mobs removed King Louis-Philippe—another ruler who wanted total power—and established the Second Republic. His successor, Napoléon III (Napoléon Bonaparte's nephew) proved no better. He led the nation to defeat in war with Germany in 1870, after which the French set up the Third Republic.

France During the World Wars

Hatred and distrust between France and Germany continued. This contributed to the outbreak of World War I in 1914. The most destructive war in history up to that time, it pitted France, Britain, Russia, and the United States against Germany, Austria, and Turkey. Much of the fighting took place in northern France. By the time the war ended in 1918, large parts of that region were in ruins, and more than 1.5 million French people had been killed.

French villagers sort through their ruined homes at the end of World War I.

Although France emerged from the war on the winning side, it had been so devastated that recovery was difficult. Thus, it was largely unprepared when Germany launched World War II in 1939. Led by the dictator

Adolf Hitler, German troops invaded and took control of northern France in 1940. Southern France was governed from a town called Vichy. The Vichy government cooperated with the Germans. By the end of 1942, the Germans occupied all of France.

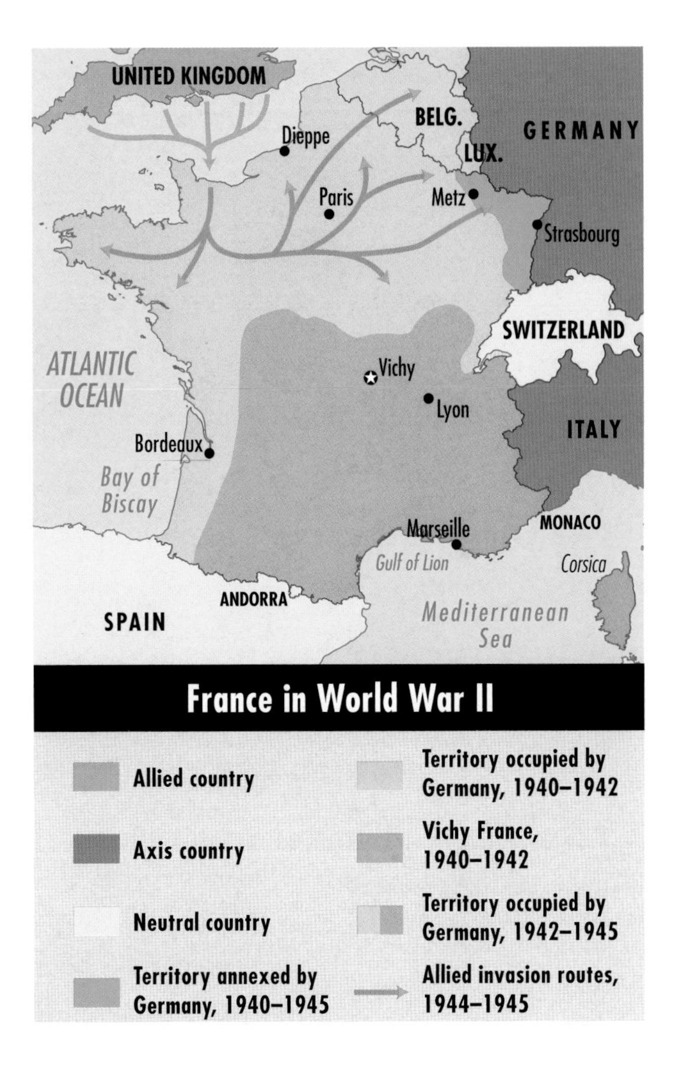

France in World War II

While the Germans controlled France, some French joined the Resistance, a group of freedom fighters who blew up factories, armories, and bridges the Germans relied on to wage war. Nevertheless, the German occupiers used French raw materials and labor to strengthen their war effort.

The beginning of the end of France's ordeal came on June 6, 1944. On that day, the United States, Britain, Canada, and France's other allies landed thousands of troops on the beaches of Normandy. They swept across France, liberating the people. Germany was defeated the following year.

The Fourth and Fifth Republics

After the war, the French established another new government—the Fourth Republic. It carried out many economic and social reforms, including allowing women to vote. The new government also made an economic agreement with

General Charles de Gaulle visits Algeria in 1959. As president, de Gaulle pushed for Algerian independence.

Belgium, Luxembourg, the Netherlands, West Germany, and Italy, called the European Economic Community (EEC), or Common Market. The EEC, founded in 1957, was designed to make it easier for Europeans to exchange goods and improve their economies and living conditions. The member countries also hoped that it would break down their old rivalries and help them to work together in peace.

France continued to have problems in other parts of the world. From the time World War II ended, the people who lived in French colonies in Asia and Africa had been rising up against the French and declaring their independence. War eventually broke out between the French army and people in Algeria, a French-controlled region in North Africa. As the crisis continued, the French people became increasingly divided over how to handle it.

In 1958, with France seemingly on the brink of civil war, the French asked Charles de Gaulle, their greatest World War II hero, to step in and resolve the crisis. He said he would if he could draft a new constitution giving him almost dictatorial powers. The people agreed, and the Fifth Republic was born. The new president did not disappoint his supporters. He worked out a peaceful settlement in Algeria, which became independent in 1962. His government also brought the nation increased economic stability and prosperity. De Gaulle resigned in 1969.

Modern French Politics

In 1981, François Mitterrand won the presidency. His government quickly imposed control over many industries, banned nuclear weapons testing, and placed heavy taxes on the rich. Mitterrand was reelected in 1988, but he became increasingly unpopular as prices and unemployment rose sharply.

François Mitterrand served as president of France from 1981 to 1995. To date, no other French president has served as long.

Campaigning on a pledge to reduce unemployment, Jacques Chirac, a conservative, won the presidency in 1995. He quickly reinstated the country's nuclear testing program. Chirac was also a strong backer of France's participation in the European Union (EU), a federation of European nations that promotes political and economic cooperation among its members. Chirac was reelected in 2002.

France remains a free and strong democracy. It took centuries of strife and hardship for France to come into being. Now, the French have entered the new century with passion, energy, and hope for the future.

A Strong Democracy

France's modern democracy arose out of political upheaval. After the end of the chaos wrought by the two world wars, the French established the Fourth Republic in 1946. Though many people had high hopes for it, the new governmental system turned out to be inefficient and unstable. The main reason was that most of the power rested in the hands of the national legislature, while the president had very little power. Legislators often changed their minds about the direction the country should be heading. In the twelve years

Opposite: **The European Union parliament meets in Strasbourg, France.**

Troyes is an ancient town on the Seine River. Its town hall dates back to the 1600s.

The National Anthem

France's stirring national anthem, "La Marseillaise," was written during the French Revolution by a French soldier named Claude-Joseph Rouget de Lisle.

French lyrics

Allons enfants de la Patrie,
Le jour de gloire est arrivé!
Contre nous de la tyrannie,
L'étendard sanglant est levé!
L'étendard sanglant est levé!
Entendez-vous dans les campagnes
Mugir ces féroces soldats?
Ils viennent jusque dans nos bras
Egorger nos fils et nos compagnes!

CHORUS:

Aux armes, citoyens!
Formez vos bataillons!
Marchons! marchons!
Qu'un sang impur
Abreuve nos sillons!

English lyrics

Arise children of the fatherland,
The day of glory has arrived!
Against us tyranny's
Bloody standard is raised!
Bloody standard is raised!
Do you hear in the fields
The howling of these fearsome soldiers?
They are coming into our midst
To cut the throats of our sons and consorts!

CHORUS:

To arms citizens!
Form your battalions!
March, march!
Let impure blood
Water our furrows!

of the Fourth Republic, the legislature replaced the country's top leaders twenty-two times!

Eventually, the French people realized that they needed a more stable kind of democracy. The popular war hero Charles de Gaulle argued that the nation needed a stronger president who could act quickly when the legislature was bogged down in argument and indecision. Most of the French people agreed with him. In 1958, they voted to adopt his new constitution, which created the Fifth Republic. This constitution remains in place today.

Ségolène Royal was the Socialist Party candidate for president in 2007. She lost to conservative candidate Nicolas Sarkozy.

Executive Power

France's government is divided into three branches: executive, legislative, and judicial. The head of the executive branch is the president. The president is both powerful and independent. Although the president belongs to a political party, he or she does not run for office as the head of that party. The president runs for office on his or her own merits and answers only to the people. French voters—men and women at least eighteen years old—elect the president every five years.

One of the president's most important duties is to appoint cabinet members. The cabinet is often referred to as "the government." Each cabinet minister is in charge of a different aspect of running the country. So, for example, there is a minister of foreign affairs, a minister of agriculture, and so on. Working with the president, France's cabinet ministers set national policies and propose new laws. The chief minister, called the prime minister, is not as powerful as the president because the president can replace the prime minister at any time.

The president also has a number of special powers. For example, the president can dissolve the elected legislature and call for new elections. The president can also call for a national referendum at any time. A national referendum is a special election in which the people vote directly on a single issue. In April 1962, Charles de Gaulle held a referendum to decide whether Algeria should become independent from France. More than 90 percent of the French people voted yes, and the matter was settled. Thus, by appealing to the people for an immediate thumbs-up or thumbs-down on an issue, the president can avoid a long political fight with the legislature. In addition, in an emergency the president can assume nearly dictatorial powers for a short time.

Charles de Gaulle wanted France to be powerful and independent. He believed that France should not have to depend on any other country for its security.

The president cannot be removed from office, except on a charge of "high treason," such as betraying the nation to a foreign enemy. In other words, the president cannot be fired for such offenses as misusing public funds or lying to the people. Some people worry that the president's powers are too great. They fear that someday a person may use these powers to become a dictator. So far, however, no one has abused the presidency in this manner, so most voters see no reason to change the system.

Man of Ambition

Some French people love President Jacques Chirac; others hate him. But they all agree that he has been one of the most ambitious French politicians of the last hundred years. Now leader of France's conservative Gaullist party, Chirac was first elected to the National Assembly in 1967. In the years that followed, he held a number of important government posts, including mayor of Paris and prime minister of the national government. In 1988, Chirac ran for the presidency and lost. But the relentlessly ambitious Chirac managed to capture France's highest office in 1995. He was reelected in 2002.

Chirac has been a big supporter of French participation in the European Union. He is also a strong advocate of national defense. In 2006, he announced that he would consider using nuclear weapons to retaliate against terrorist attacks on France.

The Legislature

The French national legislature consists of two houses, the National Assembly and the Senate. The stronger and more important of the two, the National Assembly, has 577 members who are elected directly by the people and serve for five years. Like congresspeople in the United States, members of the National Assembly propose new laws. In France, however, more than 90 percent of proposed laws come from cabinet ministers. That means that the National Assembly spends most of its time debating, changing, and voting on bills that the government sends it.

The French Senate has 321 members. This number is gradually being increased, however, and in 2010, the Senate

The French National Assembly meets in the Palais Bourbon. Assemblies have been meeting there since the late 1700s.

will have 346 members. Senators serve nine-year terms. They are elected indirectly, rather than directly by the people. The people elect various national, regional, and city officials who are called "great electors." These electors hold special meetings in which they choose the members of the Senate. Like the National Assembly, the Senate debates and changes legislation. But the Senate wields less power than the National Assembly, which can pass bills without the Senate's approval. The Senate has one unique power, though. The nation has no elected vice president, and if the president resigns or dies in office, the leader of the Senate becomes acting president until new elections can be held.

The Courts

France has criminal and civil courts in its major cities. Serious crimes punishable by more than ten years in prison are tried in Courts of Assize. These are the only French courts that have juries. Each Assize Court has nine jurors and three professional judges. All other courts in France are made up solely of judges.

If someone is not satisfied with the decision of a lower court, the case can be brought before a Court of Appeals. Rulings made by a Court of Appeals can be appealed to

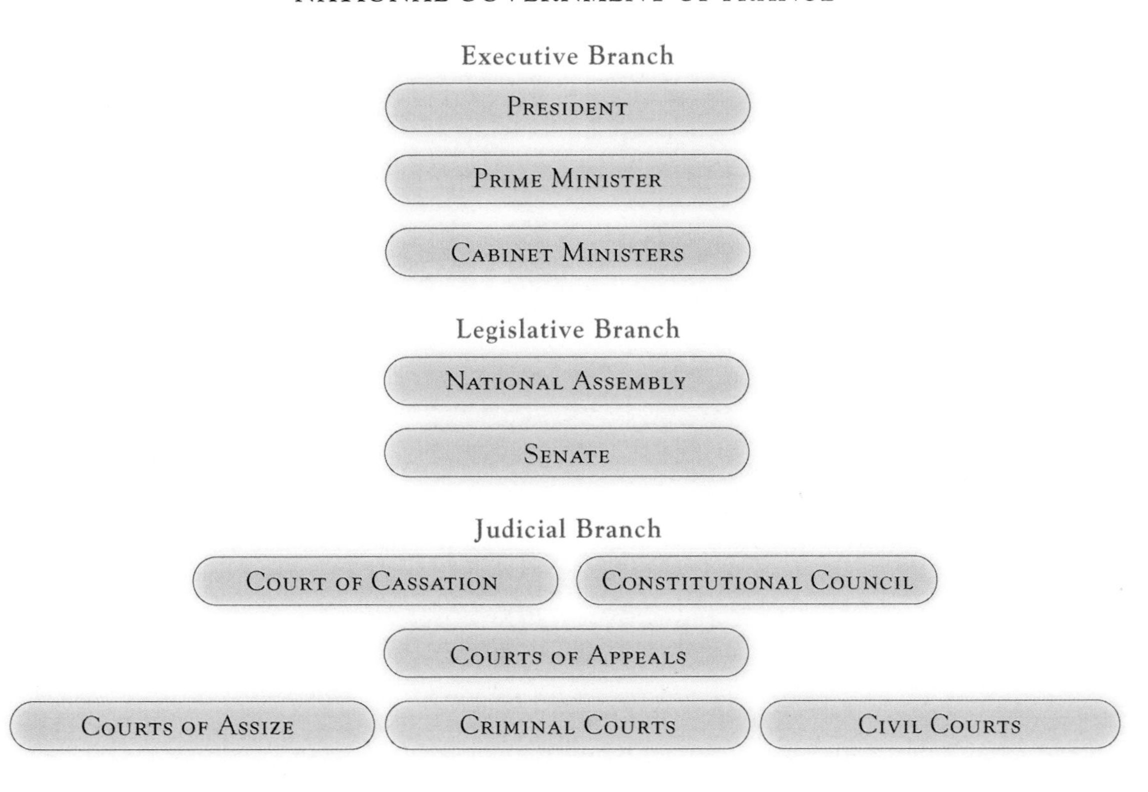

the Court of Cassation, France's highest court. Judges are appointed for life.

The Court of Cassation does not deal with questions of whether laws follow the constitution. Instead, a body called the Constitutional Council examines controversial laws before they are approved by the legislature. The Constitutional Council has nine members who serve nine-year terms. Three are appointed by the president, three by the head of the National Assembly, and three by the head of the Senate. The Constitutional Council also can declare an election invalid and call for a new one if it finds evidence of fraud.

The members of the Constitutional Council pose with President Jacques Chirac (fifth from right). Only the Constitutional Council can decide if a law violates the French Constitution.

The French Flag

France's national flag is called the "tricolor" because it features broad stripes in three colors—blue, white, and red. Red and blue were long the symbolic colors of Paris, and white was the color most often used by French royalty. During the French Revolution, the new government adopted a flag combining the three colors. The red and blue stripes enclose the white, in a sense suggesting that the people control the monarchy and therefore their own freedom.

Departments and Communes

In addition to its national government, France has regional governments somewhat like those of U.S. states. France is divided into ninety-six departments. Each department has a governor, called a prefect, who is appointed by the president's cabinet, and a general council elected by the people. Together, the prefect and the general council direct a department's affairs.

France also has about 36,500 town and city governments known as communes. The people living in each commune elect a council of officials. The officials then elect a mayor from their own ranks. Paris, France's capital city, is unusual in that it is both a department and a commune. It has a regional government, headed by a prefect, and a local government, headed by a mayor.

Paris: Did You Know This?

The capital city of France, Paris, lies on the Seine River about 90 miles (145 km) southeast of the river's mouth, on the English Channel. Paris is home to almost 2.2 million people—11.5 million counting the suburbs. It is France's largest city and the fourth-largest city in all of Europe.

Paris began in about 250 B.C. as a Celtic fishing village. It grew steadily through the centuries. The Romans, who conquered France in the late first century B.C., called the city Lutetia. But, towards the end of the Roman period, it reverted to its more ancient Gallic name, Parissi, which was later shortened to Paris. In the 500s, Paris became the capital of the Frankish king Clovis, who built the city's first cathedral. As the centuries passed, Paris continued to grow. Its greatest increase in population came in the 1800s, as industry grew.

Today, Paris is one of the world's most beautiful cities and most popular tourist destinations. The city is chock-full of fine restaurants, impressive monuments, world-class museums, and alluring neighborhoods. Each year, tens of millions of people go to Paris to crane their necks at the Eiffel Tower, marvel at the magnificent art in the Louvre, and explore the steep streets of Montmartre.

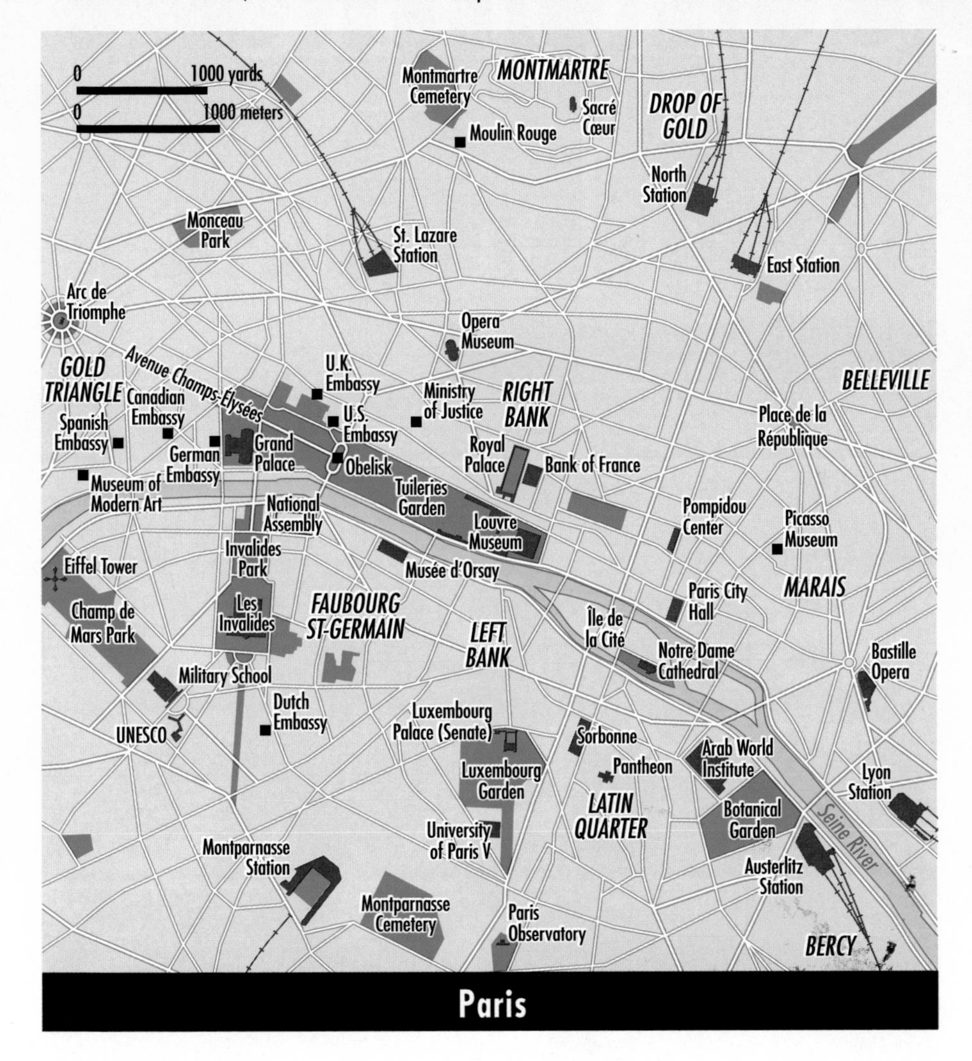

Paris

Economic Powerhouse

France has one of the world's strongest economies. The country's economy has been robust throughout much of its history. Even in ancient times, the region that is now France was an economic powerhouse. Gaul produced huge amounts of crops and livestock, supplying the Romans with much of their food. Later, mining and manufacturing developed as well, though agriculture remained the cornerstone of the economy. By the early 1700s, France was one of the world's richest nations.

Opposite: **Sunflowers are one of the leading agricultural products in central France.**

A French metalworking workshop from 1770

After World War II, the French economy increased in both size and diversity. Agriculture remained important, but an increasing number of people gave up farming for steadier, better-paying work in factories and businesses. In 1939, just before World War II, about 35 percent of French workers made their living by farming, the highest proportion in Europe. By 2006, that figure had fallen to 6 percent.

In the postwar years, both the French government and private investors put much time, effort, and money into expanding industries such as coal, natural gas, electricity, chemicals, and textiles. Production of cars, trucks, ships, and airplanes also increased. The French shipped these products

Money Facts

For more than two hundred years after the French Revolution, the basic unit of French currency was the franc. That changed in 2002, when the French adopted the euro, the currency of the European Union. Today, thirteen EU states use the euro.

On the front of each euro note is an image of a window or a gateway. On the back is a picture of a bridge. These images do not represent any actual bridges or windows. Instead, they are examples from different historical periods.

One euro is divided into one hundred cents. Bills come in values of 5, 10, 20, 50, 100, 200, and 500 euros. Coins come in values of 1 and 2 euros, as well as 1, 2, 5, 10, 20, and 50 cents. In 2007, US$1 equaled about 0.76 euro, and 1 euro equaled US$1.31.

all over the world. In 2005, France's exports were worth US$443 billion, the fifth-highest total of any country.

France's Trading Partners

About two-thirds of these exports go to France's European trade partners. The development of economic partnerships with its neighbors has provided France with ready markets for its goods and has helped the nation prosper. The first such partnership formed in 1957 when the French became part of the six-member European Economic Community (EEC). Today, the successful EEC has become the even more successful European Union (EU), with twenty-seven member countries.

The EU countries have agreed to a system of free trade. This means that no import taxes are paid on goods shipped between these countries. This keeps the cost of French products down in other EU countries.

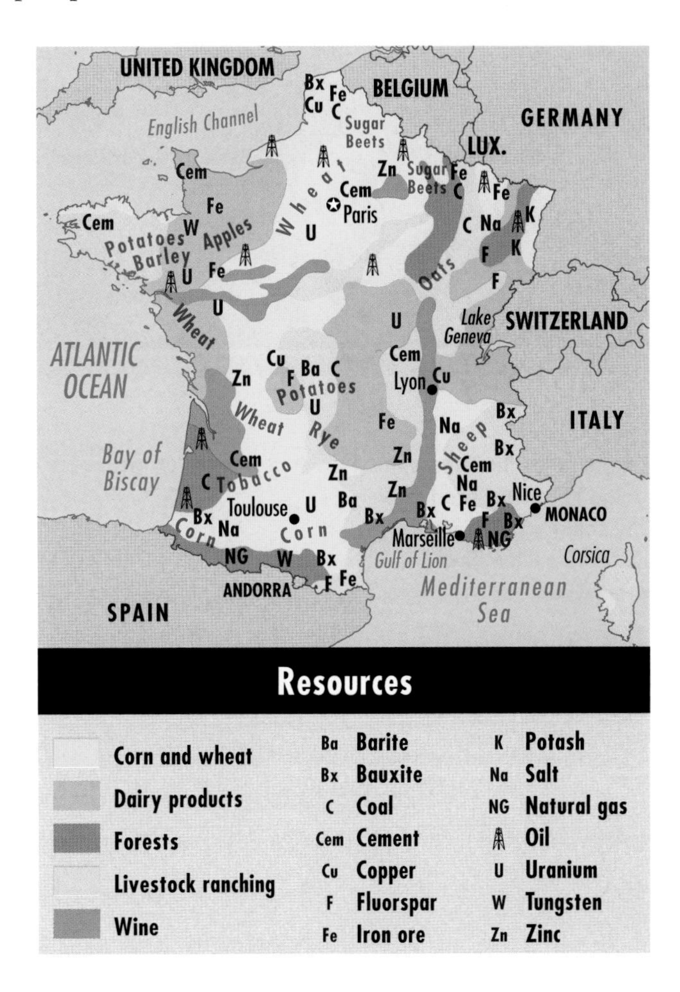

Farming in France

Slightly more than half the land in France is used for agriculture. Today, France has about 600,000 farms, down from about 730,000 in the mid-1990s. Yet the country's agricultural output

France leads the European Union in poultry production. The country raises nine hundred million birds every year.

has not dropped. In fact, more advanced farming methods and more effective fertilizers have actually increased the nation's agricultural output. France remains one of the world's largest exporters of farm products.

Many French farmers have begun growing new crops that are popular in foreign countries. Among these are sweet corn, sunflowers, and other crops used in making cooking oils. Meanwhile, traditional French products such as wheat, barley, sugar beets, beef, poultry, milk, and wine remain as important as ever. France ranks first in the EU in the production of sugar beets and beef and second in the world in making wine.

Diverse Factories

France's industries, like its general economy, are diverse. Iron, bauxite, potash, oil, and natural gas are all mined in France. These materials are then manufactured into usable products. For example, oil is used to produce electricity. Potash goes into chemicals and fertilizers. And French factories turn bauxite into aluminum. Other factories use the aluminum, along with steel and other materials, to make cars. Every year, France also produces ships, aircraft, and trains valued at more than US$20 billion.

One of France's main industrial zones is in the northern reaches of the Massif Central. The plateau used to be rich in minerals, including coal, copper, lead, and iron, but years of mining have depleted the deposits. Coal mining in the area

What France Grows, Makes, and Mines

Agriculture	
Wheat	38,000,000 metric tons
Sugar beets	34,000,000 metric tons
Corn	15,630,000 metric tons
Manufacturing	
Steel	18,000,000 metric tons
Cars	3,500,000 units
Chemicals	US$41,000,000,000 worth
Mining	
Natural gas	1,400,000,000 cubic meters
Coal	1,700,000 metric tons
Oil	28,357,000 barrels

The French Auto Industry

More than a century ago, the French were pioneers in car manufacturing. Today, France has the fourth-largest automobile industry in the world, turning out some six million vehicles each year. France is the site of twelve large auto manufacturing plants, which together employ more than 330,000 people. Most plants are owned by the two main French carmakers, Renault and PSA, but several foreign companies, including Toyota, Scania, and DaimlerChrysler, now have plants in France.

has been particularly hard-hit, declining by more than 50 percent since the 1950s. Some of the plateau's industrial towns, most notably Clermont-Ferrand and Saint-Étienne, are still thriving. Clermont-Ferrand not only produces many steel goods, such as airplane engines and railroad equipment, but also has one of the world's largest tire factories.

Natural-gas production is centered at Pau and Lacq, in the Pyrenees foothills in southern France. When the gas deposits

A Global Perfume Center

France is a global leader in perfume production. In 2006, it earned about US$5.8 billion from perfume. Four of the world's eight biggest-selling perfume lines are French. Among the leading perfume manufacturers is Guerlain. The company was founded in 1828, and, later in the century, it created special scents for the queens of England and Spain. Other leading French perfume companies include Caron, Chanel, Patou, and Gucci.

at Lacq were discovered in 1951, they were the second largest in Europe. Another major French industrial zone lies in the Paris region, where thousands of factories turn out clothing, cars, engineering equipment, and food products.

A Popular Tourist Destination

France has long been a popular destination for tourists from around the globe. More than sixty million foreigners visit the country's beautiful landscapes and rich cultural attractions each year. People flock to ski resorts in the Alps, beaches along the Mediterranean coast, and wine-growing valleys. They throng Paris and other cities to experience the world-famous museums, churches, and cafés.

Skiing is often a family affair in France. The Avoriaz ski resort gives lessons to children as young as three years old.

More than a million people work in France's tourist industry. Tourism brings billions of dollars a year into the country, making it one of the most important sectors of France's economy.

The French People

More than sixty million people live in France today. Generally, the areas with the most industry, business activity, or tourism have the largest and fastest-growing populations. These include the mining and industrial regions of the north and northeast, the Lyon region in the Rhône–Saône Corridor, the Côte d'Azur, and, especially, the Paris region. By contrast, areas with no industry or poor soil are sparsely populated.

Opposite: **Most Basques live in rural areas of the western Pyrenees in southern France.**

About 77 percent of French people live in urban areas.

Populations of France's Largest Cities (2005 est.)

City	Population
Paris	2,144,700
Marseille	808,700
Lyon	465,300
Toulouse	431,500
Nice	347,100

Paris spreads out on both sides of the Seine River.

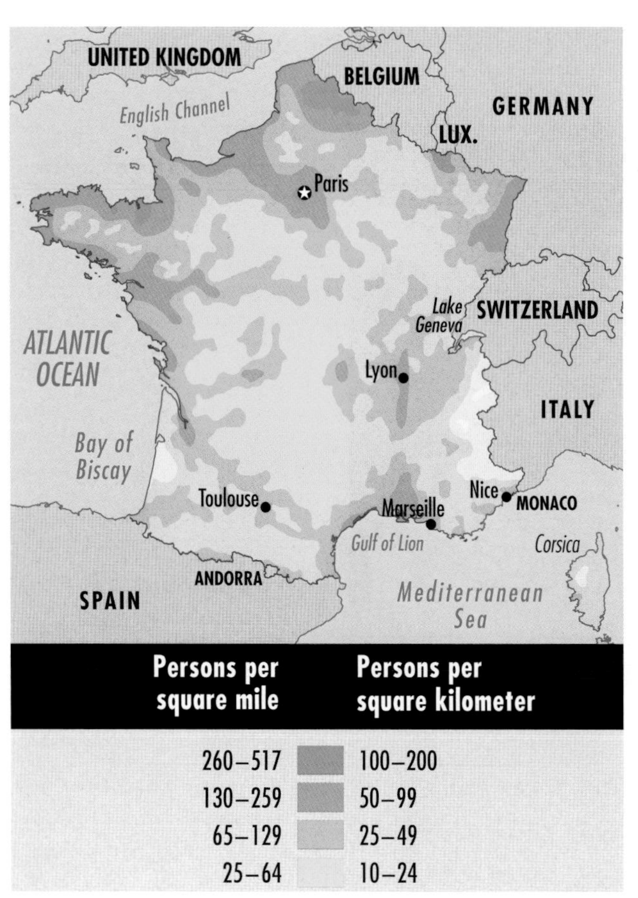

The Growth of Cities

Many French cities have grown quickly in recent decades. In 1911, the population of the Paris region was just over 5 million. By 2006, that number had more than doubled to about 11.5 million. About 2 million people live in the city of Paris, while the rest live in the surrounding suburbs. Similar growth occurred in other French cities. Overall, France experienced higher population growth, especially in urban areas, in the past five decades than any other European nation.

The flip side of this urban growth is a corresponding drop in the number of people in the rural areas. Many towns and villages shrank. Some, mostly in the Pyrenees and the Massif Central, were completely deserted. This trend slowed somewhat in the 1980s and 1990s, partly because city dwellers began buying and restoring old houses in the abandoned areas to use as vacation homes.

Origins of the French People

Many outside groups settled in France during the country's long history, so the native French have a mixed ancestry. Their ethnic origins include Celtic, Roman, German, Viking, North African, and other groups.

The origins of one group, the Basques, are particularly hard to trace. The Basques have lived in the sheltered valleys and hillsides of the western Pyrenees in southern France and northern Spain for more than two thousand years. Their language is unrelated to any European tongue. From their mountain strongholds, the Basques fought off Roman, German, Muslim, and other invaders through the centuries. They finally lost their independence to the French after the 1789 revolution. Even so, the Basques stubbornly held on to their language and customs. Today, between seventy thousand and eighty thousand people in France speak the Basque language. Their numbers drop slightly each year.

The Pyrenees are Basque country. Many signs in the region are in both French and the Basque language.

By contrast, the origins of immigrants who came to France in the twentieth century are well known. After World War II, when French industry was rapidly expanding, new factory jobs attracted many foreign workers. Among them were immigrants from Spain, Portugal, Poland, Italy, and France's former colonies in North Africa and Southeast Asia. The automobile industry in particular came to depend on these foreign workers, who were often willing to work for lower wages than French natives.

Many immigrants to France work in the auto industry.

Muslim women shopping in Paris. Some Muslims believe that women must cover their hair and wear loose clothing.

Muslim Immigration

The largest single group of immigrants to France in recent years comes from the former French colony of Algeria. Algerians and other people of North African origin now make up more than 80 percent of the five million foreign-born people living in France.

Most immigrants, especially those from other European countries, have found the French friendly and accepting. The North Africans have had a more difficult time, however. This is partly because of tensions stemming from racial and cultural differences. The North Africans are darker-skinned than most French, and most are Muslim. Also, some native-born French have accused North Africans and other immigrants of taking jobs from French people.

A burnt-out car sits in the street following the riots of 2005. The riots revealed the depth of anger and frustration in some French immigrant communities.

In the 1980s, this resentment led to the formation of a political party, the National Front Party, that wanted to stop Muslim immigration. Using the racist slogan "France for the French," the party's leader managed to win more than 14 percent of the vote in the 1988 presidential elections. Since that time, the National Front Party has lost some ground, but racial tensions persist. Some children of immigrant parents experience racial hatred even though they were born and educated in France. They also complain of unemployment and police harassment. Tensions came to a head in the fall of 2005, when Muslims rioted in towns across the country. One person was killed, several hundred were injured, and thousands of cars were burned.

Language

Because people in France come from so many different lands, it would seem that the country would have many different languages, but this is not the case. Most immigrants speak French in addition to their native tongue. French remains the nation's dominant language.

Most French people are proud of their language. The French have long recognized that spoken words change faster than written ones and that the influx of foreign words can change a language. In 1635, they established the Académie française, or French Academy, to protect the French language from such changes. It consists of forty scholars who

Signs leading to the Channel Tunnel that connects France with Great Britain are in both French and English.

Common French Words and Phrases

Bonjour	Hello
Adieu or *Au revoir*	Good-bye
S'il vous plaît	Please
Oui	Yes
Non	No
Comment ça va?	How are you?
Merci	Thank you
De rien	You're welcome
Excusez-moi.	Excuse me.
Pardon	Sorry
Je m'appelle . . .	My name is . . .

are appointed for life. They keep track of new words entering the language, decide which words should be allowed in the official dictionary, and set standards of usage. The members of the academy, along with many other French citizens, became alarmed in the twentieth century as English words and phrases became common in spoken French. This mixture of the two languages came to be called *franglais*.

Several dialects, or versions, of French are spoken around the country. In the northeastern Alsace and Lorraine regions, for example, people use a dialect that mixes in French and German. In Brittany, in the northwest, the dialect is Breton, a mixture of French and English. And in southeastern France, the site of Rome's original Gallic province, the most common dialect is Provençal, which retains many Latin influences.

French Phrases Used in English

avant-garde	ahead of its time, especially in the arts
Bon appétit!	Enjoy your meal!
C'est la vie.	That's life.
crème de la crème	the best
déjà vu	the feeling you've seen something before
esprit de corps	group spirit
faux pas	a mistake
par excellence	to the highest degree
raison d'être	a reason for existing
tour de force	an outstanding feat

Newspapers announce the results of a vote. The answer was a resounding "no."

The Elder Daughter of the Church

CHRISTIANITY TOOK HOLD IN FRANCE AFTER THE Frankish leader Clovis converted to that religion in the year 496. The French were devout Christians for so many centuries that their nation eventually came to be called *la fille aînée de l'église*, "the elder daughter of the church." Roman Catholicism was the official religion in France until 1905, when the government passed laws separating church and state.

Opposite: **Coutances Cathedral is a masterpiece of Gothic architecture.**

This painting depicts Clovis being baptized in 496.

France's Most Enduring Landmark

One of the most beautiful and imposing churches in the world, the Cathedral of Notre Dame is also France's most enduring landmark. It is located on the Île de la Cité, an island in the Seine River in the middle of Paris. Begun in 1163 and completed in 1345, the cathedral offers a magnificent view of the city from the tops of its twin towers. The best time to visit the cathedral's interior is in the early morning. Soft multicolored shafts of light that stream through the stained glass windows illuminate parts of the vast and otherwise dimly lit church. The south tower houses the cathedral's great bell, the one supposedly tolled by Quasimodo, the fictional title character in Victor's Hugo's novel *The Hunchback of Notre Dame.*

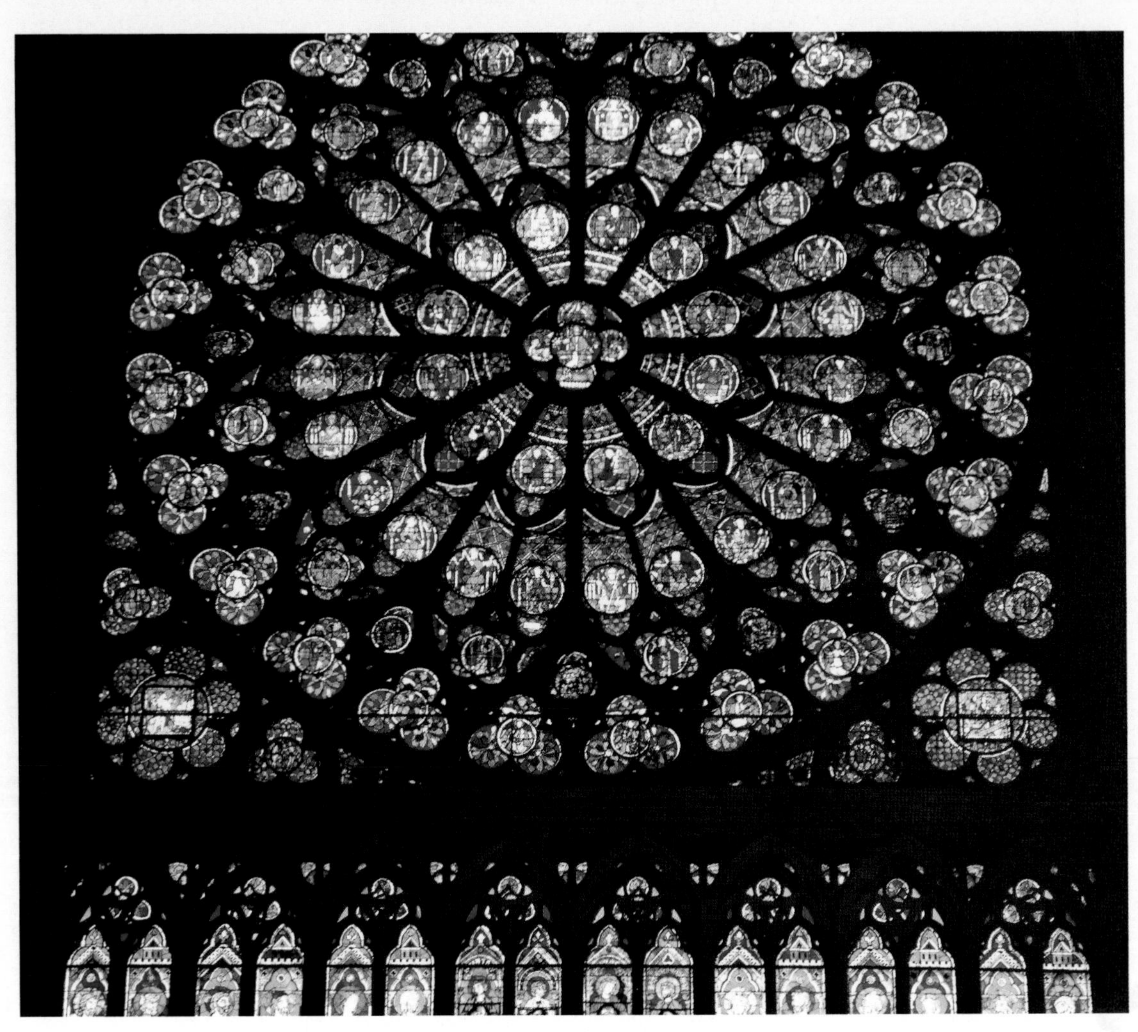

Vincent de Paul established several organizations for the poor. One was a home for abandoned babies.

Cathedrals and Saints

Until recent decades, the Roman Catholic Church, its teachings, and its clergy were guiding forces in everyday French life. Almost everyone, rich or poor, worshiped regularly and observed religious holidays. The French people also expressed their devotion to God by building magnificent churches. Among the finest are the Cathedral of Notre Dame in Paris, completed in 1345, and Chartres Cathedral, 55 miles (88 km) southwest of Paris, finished in about 1220. Chartres Cathedral has some of the finest stained glass windows in Europe.

France has also produced more than its share of saints, people the Catholic Church have judged to be especially holy. Perhaps the most famous is Joan of Arc, who was burned at the stake in 1431 on the trumped-up charge of witchcraft. The Catholic Church made her a saint in 1920. Francis de Sales (1567–1622) is best known for his writings, especially

The Miracle of Lourdes

One of the world's most famous Catholic shrines is located in southern France. In 1858, a fourteen-year-old girl named Bernadette Soubirous claimed that the Virgin Mary visited her eighteen times in a cave near Lourdes. Many people called her visions a miracle. They came to believe that the waters of a nearby stream could heal the sick.

Today, as many as five million people visit the cave at Lourdes every year. Many of them are hoping that a miracle will cure their illness.

Introduction to a Devout Life. In 1923, the Catholic Church proclaimed him the patron saint of all Catholic writers. Other memorable French religious figures are Saint Vincent de Paul (born in 1581), who was noted for his work helping the needy, and Saint Bernadette (born in 1844), who claimed that she had personal contact with the Virgin Mary, the mother of Jesus, near Lourdes.

A Religious Battleground

Because the Catholic faith was so firmly entrenched in France, the nation turned into a religious battleground when church reformers came along in the sixteenth century. The Reformation began in the 1500s, when a number of European clergymen tried to rid the Catholic Church of what they saw as corruption. One of these men was a French religious leader named John Calvin. The church strongly opposed the efforts of these reformers. Christianity was soon divided between the Catholics, who still followed the pope in Rome, and the Protestants, who no longer recognized the pope's authority.

John Calvin was trained as a lawyer, and he brought his legal reasoning to religion. He based his religious writings on logic and close analysis of the Bible.

In France, Calvin's Protestant followers were called Huguenots. Between 1562 and 1598, the Huguenots and the Catholics engaged in bloody warfare. The bloodiest battle of all was the Saint Bartholomew's Day Massacre, on August 24, 1572. On that day, troops and armed Catholics butchered thousands of Huguenots all over France.

The St. Bartholomew's Day Massacre

In 1572, France's Catholic queen mother, Catherine de Médicis, secretly plotted with a number of Catholic leaders to murder a major Huguenot leader. The assassin failed. Fearing that the Huguenots might rise up, Catherine and her supporters decided to attack first. On August 24, a holiday celebrating St. Bartholomew, Catholic troops suddenly attacked Huguenot neighborhoods in Paris and other cities, slaying thousands of men, women, and children.

The fighting finally ended in 1598, after King Henry IV, a Protestant, converted to Catholicism. But persecution of Protestants continued in the 1600s, causing more than 250,000 French Protestants to flee to England, the Netherlands, Germany, Switzerland, and other lands. Protestants, once quite numerous in France, today make up only about 2 percent of the population.

Religions of France

Religion	Percent
Roman Catholic	81%
Muslim	7%
Protestant	2%
Jewish	1%
Other	9%

Jews and Muslims

The Protestants were not the only religious minority in France to feel the sting of intolerance and persecution. Jews have lived in France since Roman times. For many centuries, French Jews, like Jewish people in other parts of Europe, were not allowed to own property or become citizens. They were also forced to live apart from Christians. In 1306, King Philip IV forced all of France's one hundred thousand Jews to leave the country. He seized their property and money.

After the French Revolution, which promoted the ideal of brotherhood, treatment of French Jews improved greatly. Though Jews were granted full civil rights, anti-Jewish prejudices remained. In the 1890s, a French army officer named Alfred Dreyfus was falsely accused of passing information to Germany. He was accused mainly because he was Jewish. Dreyfus was cleared of wrongdoing in 1906, due in large part to the efforts of writer and social critic Émile Zola.

A synagogue is a Jewish house of worship. The synagogue in Besançon, in eastern France, was first used in 1869.

The persecution of French Jews continued in the twentieth century. As many as seventy-five thousand died in German concentration camps during World War II. They had been sent to the camps with the cooperation of French officials who were working with the Germans.

Jewish life in France improved after the war. Today, French Jews number over half a million, about 1 percent of the country's population, the highest proportion in any western European nation.

The twentieth century also witnessed French distrust and intolerance of Muslims. When large numbers of Muslims from Algeria and Morocco entered France in the 1960s, they fast became the largest religious minority in the country. Today, an estimated 7 percent of the people in France are Muslim.

Muslims pray at a mosque in Lyon. In most mosques, men and women pray in separate areas.

Many French Muslims feel discriminated against. As proof, they cite the popularity in the 1980s and 1990s of the National Front Party, whose members often criticized Muslim religious practices for being "un-French." Muslims also object to a French law that prohibits children in public school from wearing anything that shows their religion. Many Muslims believe that women should always keep their hair covered. Because of this law, however, Muslim girls are not allowed to wear head scarves in school.

Church attendance in France plummeted in the twentieth century. Today, 60 percent of French people say they never go to church.

Declining Church Attendance

On the surface, France remains a Catholic country. Polls shows that more than 80 percent of French people identify themselves as Catholic. Yet only about 8 percent of French Catholics attend church services every week. By contrast, about 40 percent of the Catholics in the United States are weekly churchgoers.

The reasons for this decline are unclear. Some people say that many French have been turned off by rigid church rules. Most French, including most Catholics, feel that church leaders have no business telling them how to conduct their personal and family matters. Another reason that French churches are frequently empty is that many French Catholics choose to worship at home. Typically they meet in groups for prayer and discussion, often with no priest present. Some devout people in France fear that French Catholicism is becoming more a social tradition and less an actual belief system.

The Finer Things

ACADEMIE · NATIONALE · DE · MUSIQUE

France has influenced art and culture in Europe more than any other nation except Greece and Italy. Gothic cathedrals, which originated in northern France, can be found all over Europe. Artists from all over the world turn out paintings in the impressionist style pioneered by nineteenth-century French artists.

Opposite: **Paris is home to one of the world's most renowned opera houses.**

France gives strong support to the arts, and many French people enjoy going to museums. France has some of the finest museums in the world, most famously the Louvre, in Paris. The French also like to read and to attend concerts and films. Such cultural activities, the French will tell you, are "the finer things," which give life meaning and pleasure.

More than seven million people visit the Louvre each year.

From Notre Dame to Versailles

Gothic architecture was the first French architectural style to spread throughout Europe. Gothic cathedrals have huge naves, or central halls, with high ceilings and many stained glass windows. To keep these immense rooms from collapsing,

The cathedral in Reims was built in the 1200s and 1300s. Its pointed arches are typical of Gothic architecture.

Many people consider Chartres Cathedral the finest Gothic cathedral in France. It is both imposing and delicate.

French architects developed external supports called flying buttresses. Gothic cathedrals also feature dizzyingly tall towers decorated with sculptures, including monstrous figures called gargoyles. The first Gothic cathedrals were built in the mid-1100s in northern France. The largest and most famous stand in Paris, Chartres, Amiens, Rouen, and Reims.

The Palace of Versailles is surrounded by one of the world's largest formal gardens. The gardens spread out over about 250 acres (100 hectares).

Many magnificent palaces were erected in France in the sixteenth and seventeenth centuries. Their design was influenced by Italian styles that had developed in the 1400s. The marriage of Italian and French styles reached its climax in the late 1600s when the Palace of Versailles was built.

Master Painters and Sculptors

The French also admired Italian artists of the day. In 1666, the monarchy established the French Academy in Rome. French artists studied there under Italian masters at the French king's expense. Around the same time, France's Royal Academy of Painting and Sculpture was also founded.

In the years that followed, France produced many great painters. Jacques-Louis David became famous for his paintings

Returning to the Classics

Jacques-Louis David (1748–1825) was one of France's greatest painters. His most important contribution to the art world may have been that he influenced other artists to tackle classical themes: the stories of ancient Greece and Rome.

As a young man, David visited Rome. There, he studied the ruins and the literature of Greek and Roman civilization. He was soon making lush paintings that depicted famous events from Greek and Roman history and mythology, including *The Oath of the Horatii* (right), *The Death of Socrates,* and *The Intervention of the Sabine Women.* David also depicted important French events, notably *The Death of Marat,* which showed the revolutionary Jean-Paul Marat lying dead in a bathtub, and *Napoléon Crossing the Alps.*

with Greek and Roman themes. In the 1800s, a romantic style of painting developed in France. Works in this style portrayed heroic, emotional, and dramatic themes. The chief French romantic painter was Eugène Delacroix (1798–1863). Perhaps his most famous work, *Liberty Leading the People*, now hangs in the Louvre.

Impressionism, a new and original French art movement, arose in the second half of the nineteenth century. The impressionist style emphasizes feeling and texture rather than strict form and detail. A typical work gives a rough, sketchy, or soft-focus "impression" of a subject rather than trying to make it look like a photograph. Among the movement's founders were Pierre Auguste Renoir (1841–1919) and Claude Monet (1840–1926).

France's Greatest Sculptor

Auguste Rodin (1840–1917) is considered France's greatest sculptor. Like other impressionist artists, Rodin did not try to make his works look perfectly realistic. Instead, his sculptures have a rough, sketchy look that captures the essence of their subjects. Rodin achieved this look in his first important work, *The Man with the Broken Nose*, which he completed in 1864. His most famous work, *The Thinker*, achieves the same sketchy style. It shows a naked man sitting on a rock, seemingly lost in thought. The choice of theme was based partly on Rodin's belief that the nude human body is the noblest subject an artist can portray.

The Louvre

The largest museum in the world rests on the banks of the Seine River in the heart of Paris. Called the Louvre, it was originally erected as a fortress in the late twelfth century. Later, French kings used it as a palace, expanding it little by little. After the French Revolution, the building became a museum. Among the Louvre's thousands of objects are ancient Egyptian, Greek, and Roman artifacts, and paintings and sculptures by European masters. The most famous by far is Leonardo da Vinci's painting of a woman with a mysterious smile, the *Mona Lisa.*

Writers and Thinkers

The French have a long-standing love of language and a fascination with ideas. France's many great writers are a source of national pride, and their work has helped shape the national identity.

René Descartes was both a philosopher and a mathematician. He is considered one of the founders of geometry.

The first literary works that can be termed uniquely French were medieval romantic tales of heroic knights. The most famous is the *Chanson de Roland* (*Song of Roland*). Written by an unknown twelfth-century poet, it describes the exploits and death of one of Charlemagne's bravest knights, Sir Roland.

In the 1600s, French literature entered a golden age. The era's great tragic playwrights included Pierre Corneille (1606–1684) and Jean Racine (1639–1699). Humor was not neglected, however, as Molière (1622–1673), one of the best comic playwrights, turned out a string of hilarious masterpieces. The century also saw the emergence in France of the world's first modern philosopher, René Descartes (1596–1650). He tried to develop a method for uncovering the truth about life and the world. Descartes is most famous for his statement, "I think, therefore I am."

France's King of Comedy

Molière was the pen name of playwright Jean-Baptiste Poquelin (1622–1673). During his career, Molière wrote some of the funniest and cleverest comedies the world has ever seen. Among them are *Tartuffe* (1664), *The Doctor in Spite of Himself* (1666), and *The Imaginary Invalid* (1673). In 1665, Louis XIV made Molière's theatrical troupe an official provider of entertainment for the royal court at Versailles.

The eighteenth century brought a new interest in science and logical thought. A new breed of thinkers and writers began to question everything, including concepts of government authority, freedom, and human rights. This movement, as well as the era, became known as the French Enlightenment. One writer from the era, Voltaire (1694–1778), compared the repressive French monarchy to the more democratic British Parliament and concluded that the British system was better. Montesquieu (1689–1755) and Jean-Jacques Rousseau (1712–1778) also championed democratic ideals. Their writings inspired the leaders of both the American and the French revolutions.

Jean-Jacques Rousseau's most famous work was *The Social Contract.* In it, he explained the need for a government of laws.

The Father of Science Fiction

Jules Verne (1828–1905) was one of France's most imaginative writers. During his long career, he wrote vivid stories that foresaw the development of space flight, submarine warfare, and skyscrapers. Along with England's H. G. Wells, Verne was one of the fathers of science fiction. His most famous novels—*Journey to the Center of the Earth* (1864), *From the Earth to the Moon* (1865), *Twenty Thousand Leagues Under the Sea* (1870), and *Around the World in Eighty Days* (1872)—all later became successful motion pictures. For reasons that remain somewhat unclear, Verne placed the manuscript for one of his most imaginative works, *Paris in the 20th Century*, in a safe and left it there. It was rediscovered by his great-grandson in 1989 and finally published in 1994.

A number of great novelists arose in the 1800s. The master of the historical novel was Victor Hugo (1802–1885). His *Hunchback of Notre Dame* (1831), about a deformed bell-ringer's love for a gypsy girl, captured life in medieval Paris. Gustave Flaubert (1821–1880), Émile Zola (1840–1902), and others turned out realistic contemporary novels. At the same time, Jules Verne helped pioneer the new literary genre of science fiction with popular novels like *Twenty Thousand Leagues Under the Sea*.

In the twentieth century, French writers continued to innovate and to influence writers in other countries. Among them were writers like Jean-Paul Sartre (1905–1980) and Albert Camus (1913–1960), whose works stress life's more absurd and meaningless aspects.

Musicians and Filmmakers

France has given the world splendid music. Perhaps the greatest French composer was Hector Berlioz (1803–1869). Many of his works, including the *Symphonie Fantastique* and *Harold in Italy*, have become modern classics. One of his most popular works, especially in France, is a new arrangement of France's national anthem. Another important French composer is Georges Bizet (1838–1875), who wrote the opera *Carmen* (1875).

Hector Berlioz was famed for his ability to express ideas through music. Many of his works were based on literature.

When they are not strolling through museums, sitting in concert halls, or curling up with a good book, many French people are at the movies. In France, the average person sees at least one film a week.

Going to the movies has a long tradition in France. In 1895, Louis and Auguste Lumière, the inventors of the film projector, gave the world's first public screening of a motion picture, in

The Lumière brothers at work in their laboratory. They invented an early type of color photography and an early motion picture camera.

The Most Popular Actor

Over the past century, France has produced many fine actors and actresses. One of the best working today is Gérard Dépardieu (1948–). Dépardieu is a stocky, tough-looking man with strong, expressive features. He has played a wide range of characters, including the title role in *Cyrano de Bergerac* (1990), for which he won a César, the French version of the Oscar. He has also appeared in several American films, including *Green Card* (1990) and *The Man in the Iron Mask* (1998).

Paris. Since that time, France has produced hundreds of great film directors and actors. The most popular actor in recent years has been the hulking and hugely talented Gérard Dépardieu.

Unlike American movies, which often emphasize action and spectacle, French movies tend to deal with human problems and relationships. But the French like American movies, too, which they watch in English with French subtitles.

The Good Life

Though Paris and other French cities are filled with apartment buildings, most people in France prefer to live in a house. In recent decades, sprawling suburbs have grown up around cities. Today, about 60 percent of French people live in houses. In fact, many French people own more than one home. Most second homes are in quiet country villages where their owners can escape the hustle and bustle of the city.

Opposite: **A rural Frenchman**

Country houses are popular among the French.

Time Off

One thing almost all French people have in common, whether they live in the city or in the country, in a high-rise apartment or in a quaint country cottage, is a lot of leisure time. In 2000, the government reduced the workweek from thirty-nine to thirty-five hours. French workers also get at least five weeks of paid vacation each year, and the legal retirement age is sixty, compared with sixty-five in the United States.

What do the French do with their spare time? Like people in North America, they spend a lot of it watching television,

Biking is an ideal way to see the French countryside.

Pet Lovers

The French are avid animal lovers, and France has the highest percentage of homes with pets in Europe. One out of three French homes has a dog. In Paris, there are more dogs than children. Cats are also popular, as are fish, hamsters, and parrots.

Not surprisingly, this love of animals has generated an enormous pet supply industry in the country. It has also resulted in a custom rarely seen in the United States—dog and cat owners bring their pets into stores and restaurants.

an average of three and a quarter hours a day. They also read and go to movies, concerts, plays, operas, museums, and sports events. Other common pastimes include fishing, hunting, hiking, and gardening.

Tarts, which are like pies without top crusts, are common in French cooking. They are filled with fruit, onions, or, in this case, eggs.

Mealtime

The French devote considerable time to preparing and eating their meals. French cooking is famous the world over. The French consider a well-prepared, unhurried meal to be one of life's greatest pleasures.

This has long included a gourmet cooking style called *haute cuisine* ("high cooking"). Haute cuisine is characterized by rich foods made with lots of butter, cream, eggs, and spices. Another cooking style—*la nouvelle cuisine* ("new cooking")—has become popular in recent years. Nouvelle cuisine uses less fat and more vegetables and fruits. Fast-food restaurants, inspired by American companies such as McDonalds, have also gained popularity in France, particularly among young people. In France, they are called *le fast-food.*

Although many busy people frequently grab fast food to save time, most French people still look forward to home-cooked meals. In order to make sure the ingredients are as fresh as possible, the average family does at least some food shopping every day. Although there are large supermarkets, most French people prefer to shop in small specialty stores. One of these is the *boucherie*, where a butcher cuts meats exactly as the customer requests. Another is the *crémerie*, which carries a large variety of cheeses. Other specialty shops include the *charcuterie*, a deli that sells salads and meat pies; the *boulangerie*, or bakery; and the *pâtisserie*, or pastry shop.

The French expect their food to be fresh. Many stop at the butcher every day.

Making Dessert

One of France's popular desserts is poached cherries in vanilla and lemon syrup.

Ingredients

3 cups water

¾ cup sugar

1 vanilla bean

zest of one lemon

1¼ lbs. cherries, pitted

1 tablespoon fresh lemon zest

Directions

Combine the water, sugar, vanilla bean, and lemon zest in a saucepan. Place over low heat and stir until the sugar dissolves. Raise the heat to high and bring the syrup to a boil. Stir in the cherries and the lemon juice. Cover the cherries with a lid slightly smaller than the saucepan to keep the cherries submerged in the syrup. Reduce the heat to low and cook for about 8 minutes. Allow the cherries to cool in the syrup, still covered. Transfer to a serving bowl, cover, and chill for at least 30 minutes before serving.

Poached cherries can be served alone or with whipped cream. They can also be used as a delicious topping for cake or ice cream.

Brioche bread is made with lots of eggs and butter. It is delicious as part of a dessert.

In France, breakfast, called *le petit déjeuner*, is most often quick and light. It usually consists of some bread or a croissant, with butter and jam, washed down with a cup of coffee, tea, or chocolate. Lunch, *le déjeuner*, used to be the largest meal. It has recently been giving way to dinner, *le dîner*, because workers' lunch hours are shorter than they once were, so they have less time to enjoy lengthy noon meals. But for Sunday lunch, family and friends gather to enjoy leisurely food and conversation.

Fewer and fewer French couples are getting married. Marriage rates have dropped 30 percent in the last twenty years.

Marriage and Children

Many French couples have two separate marriage ceremonies. The civil ceremony, which is required by law, usually takes place at the local city hall. If the couple wants a church ceremony too, it comes after the civil one.

In France, getting married is not viewed as such a life-altering step as it is in the United States. Having children, however, *is* considered life-altering, because it brings heavy responsibilities.

Having children also establishes a family. In France, the family is the most important social unit. In fact, the government pays a monthly allowance to each family based on the number of children it has. Extended families, including grandparents, aunts, uncles, and cousins, are usually close and supportive.

The French view childrearing as an important job, and French parents and other relatives watch their children's behavior closely. Adults are not shy about disciplining children in public. This is because adults feel it is their duty to civilize young people and help them become responsible members of society.

The baccalauréat exams at the end of lycée (high school) cover subjects such as literature, science, history, and geography.

Schools

French children are well educated. French parents are concerned with making sure their children study hard and get good grades. They know that those who do well in school often get the best jobs and make higher salaries later in life. It is also important to the French, young and old alike, to appear literate, cultured, and well-spoken.

French children put in long hours of study, in school and at home. On average, classes begin between eight and eight-thirty in the morning and end between four and four-thirty in the afternoon. When they get home, most children are expected to complete their homework before dinner. Although French students have many school vacations, they are assigned lengthy "vacation homework."

Most French children attend nursery school before they are six years old. From ages six to eleven they go to primary school, after which they have four years of junior high. At age sixteen, they can either quit school or pursue higher learning. Those who do continue on enter a *lycée*, a high school that prepares them to take the *baccalauréat*, or "*bac*," a difficult university entrance exam. Students who pass the bac (about one-third of the students fail it) enroll in one of France's more than seventy universities or in one of its special colleges that prepare people for careers in politics, law, or business. All forms of higher education in France are paid for by the government, so no tuition is charged.

College students in Strasbourg enjoy a conversation. More foreign students go to college in France than in any other country in the European Union.

The Joys of Rugby

Rugby is popular among French people of all ages. A rugby ball is shaped somewhat like an American football. The two games have a number of differences, however.

In rugby, the players do not wear heavy padding, as American football players do. As in football, the main object is to carry the ball over the opposing team's goal line. Players advance the ball by running with it, kicking it, or passing it, though no forward passes are allowed in rugby. Also, rugby play is continuous. The game stops only when the ball goes out of bounds or someone breaks a rule.

Popular Sports

Although French children study long and hard, they find ample time for sports. They play some sports at school. Between classes, students play volleyball, gymnastics, and soccer. Many schools also sponsor one-week stays at the seashore or in the mountains. On these retreats, students still attend classes, but they also learn to swim or ski.

Still, sports are less of a national obsession in France than they are in some countries, like the United States and Canada. In general, the French prefer playing and watching individual sports, particularly skiing, cycling, and swimming, to team sports. The main exceptions are rugby and soccer. The national soccer championships are one of three biggest sporting events in France. The other two are the Tour de France, a long cross-country bicycle race, and the Grand Prix car races held at Le Mans.

The World's Greatest Bicycle Race

Since the Tour de France was established in 1903, it has been the world's most popular and prestigious bicycle race. Each July, tens of thousands of spectators line roadways, and millions more watch it on TV. During the event, about two hundred cyclists pedal madly across the French countryside, covering about 2,300 miles (3,700 km) in three weeks. The winner receives a prize of 450,000 euros (about US$600,000) and worldwide acclaim. American Lance Armstrong won the race seven years in a row, from 1999 to 2005.

The Art of Talking

The French follow certain verbal rules that can appear strange to foreigners. For example, when entering a shop, you are expected to say hello (*bonjour*) to the owner or clerk. In fact, it is considered rude not to do so. Likewise, you should say thank you (*merci*) and good-bye (*au revoir*) when leaving the shop, even if you did not buy anything.

The French consider conversation both a skill and an art. To foreigners, French conversations can seem like heated arguments. But such exchanges are rarely angry. They are better described as "spirited but friendly" attempts to exchange opinions. They follow certain rules that all French people know and accept as polite.

French teenagers at a shoe store. The lives of French teens are much like those of North American teens.

Conversation is a great pleasure of French life.

The most important rule of conversation in France is to choose an acceptable topic. The French seldom, if ever, engage in idle chatter about the weather or their personal problems. They consider visitors who do engage in such chatter to be shallow, boring, or both. They frown on discussing money and consider it impolite to ask people what they do for a living. More accepted topics of conversation in France are politics, food and wine, and the merits of different artists, singers, and actors. In other words, the topic should have substance and be worth arguing about.

The French also have their own way of communicating without words. Tourists sometimes cause offense by using the wrong gesture or facial expression. Smiling is a common example. Americans tend to smile a lot when traveling abroad, assuming it is a universal sign of friendliness. In France, however, smiling without a good reason, especially at a stranger, is often viewed as unpleasant, suspicious, or even idiotic. The French enjoy smiling, but they usually wait until they have a good reason.

National Holidays

New Year's Day	January 1
Easter Monday	March or April
Labor Day	May 1
1945 Victory Day	May 8
Ascension Day	40 days after Easter
Whit Monday	50 days after Easter
Bastille Day	July 14
Assumption	August 15
All Saints' Day	November 1
Armistice Day	November 11
Christmas	December 25

Timeline

French History		World History	
Cro-Magnons make hundreds of paintings in the Lascaux Caves.	ca. 15,000 B.C.		
		2500 B.C.	Egyptians build the pyramids and the Sphinx in Giza.
Celtic tribes migrate from central Europe to France.	1000 B.C.		
		563 B.C.	The Buddha is born in India.
Celts found a village that will become Paris.	250 B.C.		
The Romans conquer Gaul (France).	58–52 B.C.		
		A.D. 313	The Roman emperor Constantine legalizes Christianity.
Clovis establishes the Frankish Kingdom.	Late A.D. 400s		
		610	The Prophet Muhammad begins preaching a new religion called Islam.
Frankish leader Charles Martel defeats an invading Muslim army near Tours.	732		
Charlemagne is crowned emperor by the pope.	800		
		1054	The Eastern (Orthodox) and Western (Roman Catholic) Churches break apart.
		1095	The Crusades begin.
		1215	King John seals the Magna Carta.
		1300s	The Renaissance begins in Italy.
The Hundred Years' War begins.	1337		
		1347	The plague sweeps through Europe.
Joan of Arc leads an army that frees Orléans from the English.	1429		
Charles VII drives the English out of France.	1453	1453	Ottoman Turks capture Constantinople, conquering the Byzantine Empire.
		1492	Columbus arrives in North America.
		1500s	Reformers break away from the Catholic Church, and Protestantism is born.
French explorer Jacques Cartier makes his first voyage to Canada.	1534		
Louis XIV begins his 72-year reign.	1643		

French History

1789 The French Revolution begins.

1799 Napoléon Bonaparte comes to power.

1815 Napoléon is defeated.

1914 France enters World War I.

1940 Germany invades France in World War II.

1957 France and other countries form the European Economic Community.

1962 France grants Algeria independence.

1992 France and other countries form the European Union.

1994 A tunnel is completed under the English Channel, linking France and England.

1995 Jacques Chirac is elected president.

2003 A heat wave kills some 14,800 French.

2005 French Muslims riot over unfair treatment.

World History

1776 The U.S. Declaration of Independence is signed.

1789 The French Revolution begins.

1865 The American Civil War ends.

1879 The first practical light bulb is invented.

1914 World War I begins.

1917 The Bolshevik Revolution brings communism to Russia.

1929 A worldwide economic depression begins.

1939 World War II begins.

1945 World War II ends.

1957 The Vietnam War begins.

1969 Humans land on the Moon.

1975 The Vietnam War ends.

1989 The Berlin Wall is torn down as communism crumbles in Eastern Europe.

1991 The Soviet Union breaks into separate states.

2001 Terrorists attack the World Trade Center in New York City and the Pentagon in Washington, D.C.

Fast Facts

Official name: French Republic
Capital: Paris
Official language: French

Paris

France's flag

The Pyrenees

Official religion:	None
National anthem:	"La Marseillaise"
Type of government:	Democratic republic
Chief of state:	President
Head of government:	Prime minister
Area:	212,918 square miles (551,458 sq km)
Coordinates of geographic center:	46°00' N, 2°00' E
Dimensions:	North–south, 590 miles (950 km) East–west, 605 miles (974 km)
Bordering countries:	Spain, Andorra, and Monaco to the south; Italy, Switzerland, and Germany to the east; and Luxembourg and Belgium to the northeast
Highest elevation:	Mont Blanc, 15,771 feet (4,807 m)
Lowest elevation:	Sections of the Rhône River, 7 feet (2 m) below sea level
Average high temperatures:	Paris: 76°F (24°C) in July, 45°F (7°C) in January Nice: 81°F (27°C) in July, 55°F (13°C) in January
Average annual rainfall:	Brest (Atlantic coast): 45 inches (114 cm) Marseille (Mediterranean coast): 22 inches (56 cm)
National population (2006 est.):	60,876,136

Chartres Cathedral

Currency

Population of largest cities (2005 est):

City	Population
Paris	2,144,700
Marseille	808,700
Lyon	465,300
Toulouse	431,500
Nice	347,100

Famous landmarks:

- ***Eiffel Tower***, Paris
- ***Louvre***, Paris
- ***Cathedral of Notre Dame***, Paris
- ***Palace of Versailles***, Versailles
- ***Chartres Cathdral***, Chartres

Industry: France has a diverse economy. It mines natural gas, iron, bauxite, potash, and other minerals, which are used to manufacture steel, aluminum, cars, ships, airplanes, chemicals, fertilizers, and other products. The world's fifth-largest exporter, France shipped goods worth $443 billion to other countries in 2005. France is a major exporter of farm products, including wheat, sugar beets, corn, beef, poultry, milk, and wine.

Currency: France's basic unit of currency is the euro. In 2007, US$1 equaled 0.76 euros, and 1 euro equaled US$1.31.

Weights and measures: Metric system

Literacy: 99%

Common words and phrases:

Bonjour	Hello
Adieu or *Au revoir*	Good-bye
S'il vous plaît	Please
Oui	Yes

Talking in a café

Napoléon Bonaparte

Non	No
Comment ça va?	How are you?
Merci	Thank you
De rien	You're welcome
Excusez-moi.	Excuse me.
Pardon	Sorry
Je m'appelle . . .	My name is . . .

Famous French people:

Napoléon Bonaparte (1769–1821)
Emperor

John Calvin (1509–1564)
Religious leader

Jacques Cartier (1491–1557)
Explorer

Charlemagne (742–814)
Emperor

Charles de Gaulle (1890–1970)
Military leader, president

René Descartes (1596–1650)
Philosopher

Victor Hugo (1802–1885)
Writer

Joan of Arc (1412–1431)
Saint, national heroine

Louis XIV (1638–1715)
King

Charles Martel (686–741)
Frankish ruler

Molière (Jean-Baptiste Poquelin) (1622–1673)
Playwright

Claude Monet (1840–1926)
Painter

Pierre Auguste Renoir (1841–1919)
Painter

To Find Out More

Books

- Bull, Angela. *Joan of Arc*. New York: Dorling Kindersley, 2000.
- Dunn, John M. *The French Revolution: The Fall of the Monarchy*. San Diego: Lucent Books, 2003.
- *France* (Eyewitness Travel Guides). London: Dorling Kindersley, 2006.
- Jett, Stephen C. *France*. Philadelphia: Chelsea House Publishers, 2004.
- Mason, Antony. *In the Time of Renoir*. Brookfield, CT: Copper Beech Books, 2001.
- Prosser, Robert. *France*. New York: Facts on File, 2003.
- Sommers, Michael A. *France: A Primary Source Cultural Guide*. New York: PowerPlus, 2005.

Videos

- ***The Hunchback of Notre Dame.*** RKO, 1939.
  The best of many film versions of Victor Hugo's classic novel about Quasimodo, a deformed bell-ringer who lives in the famous Paris cathedral.
- **Visions of France.** Acorn Media, 2006.
  Spectacular images of some of France's prettiest regions.

Web Sites

- **Lost in France**
  http://www.lost-in-france.com/
  For practical information about France, French culture, and living in France.

- **Paris.org**
  http://www.paris.org
  To find out about the city's monuments, museums, stores, hotels, restaurants, and much more.

- **The World Factbook: France**
  https://www.cia.gov/cia/publications/factbook/geos/fr.html
  To find statistics and other quick information about France collected by the U.S. government.

Organizations and Embassies

- **French Embassy**
  4101 Reservoir Rd., N.W.
  Washington, D.C. 20007
  202/944-6000
  http://www.info-france-usa.org

- **French Embassy in Canada**
  42 Sussex Drive
  Ottawa, Ontario
  K1M 2C9
  613/789-1795
  http://www.ambafrance-ca.org/sommaire.php3?id_rubrique=2

- **La Maison Française**
  French Government Tourist Office
  4101 Reservoir Rd., N.W.
  Washington, D.C. 20007
  202/944-6090
  http://www.la-maison-francaise.org

Index

Page numbers in *italics* indicate illustrations.

Meet the Author

Don Nardo is a historian and award-winning writer. His specialty is ancient civilizations, particularly ancient Greece and Rome. He has traveled widely in Europe and studied firsthand many of the ancient sites he writes about. His books about French history include *Caesar's Conquest of Gaul*, *The Trial of Joan of Arc*, and *The French Revolution*.

"It was my interest in Roman France, Joan's exploits, and the turbulent revolutionary period," he says, "that made me decide to do this book about France for the Enchantment of the World series. Building on my knowledge of these phases of French history, I consulted several noted French history texts, as well as a number of volumes about the country's geography, culture, and customs. Almanacs, encyclopedias, travel guides, Internet Web sites, and telephone calls to French embassies and cultural organizations also provided much useful information. During this research, my ability to speak and read a little French came in handy."

Nardo grew up in Massachusetts. He studied theater at Syracuse University and made his living as an actor for some years before returning to college to get his history degree. He then taught high school for eight years while writing part time, before becoming a full-time writer in the mid-1980s. Since then, he has published more than three hundred books, mostly for young people and college students. He has also written several screenplays and teleplays, including work for ABC-TV. Nardo and his wife, Christine, live in Massachusetts.

Photo Credits

Photographs © 2008: **age fotostock:** 35 (Henry Ausloos), 101 (Manfred Baumann), 24 (Achim Bednorz/Bildarchiv Monheim), 61 (Henry Beeker), 99 (Wojtek Buss), 18 (J.D. Dallet), 14, 27, 94, 131 bottom (Danilo Donadoni/Marka), 25 bottom, 90, 104 (Sylvain Grandadam), 7 bottom, 29, 34, 40, 97 (Franck Guiziou/hemis), 116 (Palomba/AgenceImages), 60 (Jose Fuste Raga), 79 (Philippe Renault/hemis), 76 (Targa), 100 (Vidler/mauritius images), 7 top, 20 (R. Wacongne/AgenceImages)

Alamy Images: 37 (AA World Travel Library), 115 (Bill Bachmann), 15 (BL Images Ltd.), 30 (Michael Busselle), 127, 133 top (David R. Frazier Photolibrary, Inc.), 119 (Kevin Galvin), 107 top (Steve Nichols), 33 (Annette Price/H20 Photography), 36 top (Robert Reis), 83 (Stephen Saks Photography), 87 (Peter Titmuss), 95 (ZEVART Collection)

AP Images: 86 (Jacques Brinon), 125 (Peter Dejong), 89 (Michael Spingler)

Art Resource, NY: 44 (Bridgeman-Giraudon), 13, 52, 105 (Erich Lessing), 41, 54 (Réunion des Musées Nationaux), 107 bottom (Scala), 106 (Vanni)

Corbis Images: 55 bottom, 133 bottom (Austrian Archives), 117 (Fernando Bengoechea/Beateworks), 112 (Bettmann), 110 (Stefano Bianchetti), 9 (Massimo Borchi/Atlantide Phototravel), 103, 132 top (Charles Bowman/Robert Harding World Imagery), 64 (Henri Bureau/Sygma), 113 (Stephane Cardinale/People Avenue), 109 top (Gianni Dagli Orti), 58 (Alain Dejean/Sygma), 98 (Pascal Deloche/Godong), 91 (Philippe Eranian), 66, 80 (Owen Franken), 102 (Ian Griffiths/Robert Harding World Imagery), 73 (Historical Picture Archive), 56, 111 (Hulton-Deutsch Collection), 96 (Johansen Krause/Archivo Iconografico, SA), 42 (Francis G. Mayer/Bettmann), 45, 93 (Michael Nicholson), 63 (Alain Nogues), 114 (Doug Pearson/JAI), cover, 6 (Sergio Pitamitz), 121 (Stephane Ruet/Sygma), 65 (Reuters), 49 (Stapleton Collection), 2 (Ruth Tomlinson/Robert Harding World Imagery), 59 (Jean-Michel Turpin/Sygma)

Digital Light Source: 92 (Jacob Hutchings Photography), 74, 132 bottom (Nick Saraco Photography)

Getty Images: 25 top (Kenneth Garrett/National Geographic), 21 (Pascal Guyot/AFP), 84 (Pascal Guyot/Image Forum/AFP), 123 (Bob Handelman/Stone), 22 (Robert Harding/Digital Vision), 36 bottom (Daniel Janin/Image Forum/AFP), 78 (Alain Jocard/Image Forum/AFP), 124 (Damien Meyer/AFP), 68 (Mousse/Image Forum/AFP), 120 (Ian O'Leary/Doring Kindersley)

MapQuest.com, Inc.: 69, 131 top

Masterfile: 28 (Miles Ertman), 70 (WireImageStock), 82 top, 130 left (Jeremy Woodhouse)

Minden Pictures/Rinie Van Meurs/Foto Natura: 31

Nature Picture Library Ltd./Martin Gabriel: 39

Photolibrary/Jacques Loic: 122

Robert Fried Photography: 8, 17, 19, 38, 81, 85, 118, 126

Superstock, Inc./Steve Vidler: 23, 72

The Art Archive/Picture Desk: 48 (Bibliothèque Nationale Paris), 10 (Gianni Dagli Orti/Bibliothèque des Arts Décoratifs Paris), 109 bottom (Gianni Dagli Orti/Musée du Château de Versailles), 51, 108 (Gianni Dagli Orti/Musée du Louvre Paris)

Maps by XNR Productions, Inc.